AN EYE FOR AN I

An Eye for an I

Growing Up with Blindness, Bigotry,
and Family Mental Illness

James Francisco Bonilla

University of Minnesota Press
Minneapolis
London

A previous version of chapter 26 was published in *Creative Wisconsin Magazine* (September 2023), Wisconsin Writers Association. A previous version of chapter 31 was published in *Play Outdoors Magazine* 4, issue 4 (Spring 2024), B. Dietz Consulting Inc., Kelowna, British Columbia, Canada. A previous version of chapter 40 was published in *COLORS* 4, no. 3 (May–June 1995), Minneapolis, Minnesota.

Published by the University of Minnesota Press
111 Third Avenue South, Suite 290
Minneapolis, MN 55401-2520
http://www.upress.umn.edu

ISBN 978-1-5179-1914-6 (pb)

A Cataloging-in-Publication record for this book is available from the Library of Congress.

Printed in the United States of America on acid-free paper

The University of Minnesota is an equal-opportunity educator and employer.

34 33 32 31 30 29 28 27 26 25   10 9 8 7 6 5 4 3 2 1

Contents

Introduction

I was born with congenital cataracts, a condition experienced by only four of every ten thousand children born in the United States each year. Up to the age of nine I functioned with no sight in my left eye but with usable sight in my right. Thanks to the innate adaptability of children, I rarely felt "handicapped" (a term we'll explore later) by my lack of depth perception or limited peripheral vision. For me, that was my normal. But my life was far from normal.

At nine, I was kicked out of parochial school and shipped off to a Catholic boarding/reform school. While there, I lost much of the remaining sight in my right eye, my one good eye, as a consequence of a racially motivated assault. I was left unable to read the giant **E** in the optometrist's office, even with corrective lenses. In short, I became legally blind.

I spent the following decade, from nine to nineteen, as a New York Puerto Rican kid fighting schoolyard bullies and institutions that claimed to "rehabilitate" the visually impaired. At a very young age, I also came face to face with my family's struggles with mental illness, especially my mother's. *An Eye for an I* features themes of generational trauma, racial and sexual assault, and suicidal ideation. Please read with care. Several names have been changed to protect people's privacy. At the end of the book, in "Resources: Seeing Beyond Our Blind Spots," I offer suggested readings and videos for those seeking to address the issues raised throughout my story.

My path toward healing began with Mother Earth via transcendent encounters with a saltmarsh, a red-tailed hawk, and timber

Me, 1959.

wolves, to mention just a few. My healing continued when I was drawn into the early struggles for disability rights as well as the emerging environmental and economic justice movements. At nineteen, a breakthrough in medical technology restored the sight to my right eye.

After the events described in this memoir, I earned a doctorate in social justice education at the University of Massachusetts Amherst, and I enjoyed a career as a professor and national consultant on institutional change and cultural competence. I also spent two decades helping restore my and my wife's 1876 farmhouse and our lands back to native prairies and woodlands. I became a self-described "green multiculturalist," involved in safeguarding Mother Earth while also supporting people in developing their insights and skills in multicultural competence.

An Eye for an I is my journey in search of independence, reconciliation, and belonging. Ultimately it is an account of eyesight lost, vision restored, and insights gained. It is the story of how an instinct for survival combined with finding community, fighting for fairness, and opening to nature helped heal a spirit wounded by trauma. The therapist Galit Atlas writes, "Trauma is transmitted through our minds and our bodies, but so are resilience and healing." To that I would add one more element: hope. It's my fervent wish that you find *An Eye for an I* to be a hopeful story.

1. The Knife

I'M FIVE YEARS OLD and being chased around our tiny one bed-room apartment in Forest Hills, New York, by my knife-wielding mother. I can't recall the infraction that incited this particular frenzy, but Dinorah's rages are many and legendary. As I dodge and weave away from the contorted, angry visage that barely resembles my mother, I wonder, *Would she really stab me?*

Finally, she corners me in our long, narrow kitchen. Inching closer, she's swearing and threatening to kill me alternately in Spanish and English. The only avenue of escape left is the kitchen window, which opens outward. Unsure if she plans on spearing her only child like a pork chop, I hop onto the inside window ledge. In response she screams like a banshee. My hand flies to the window latch and, pushing it open and out, I leap with barely a hesitation.

Falling, falling, falling, I land and then tuck and roll onto a weed-infested patch of grass five feet below. Not looking back, I take off running. Unsure of where to go, I madly dash around to the back of our building and to the outside door of the apartment of Mrs. Zack, the building superintendent's wife. She often takes care of me when my regular babysitters call in sick or quit without notice. My mother's temper has made keeping childcare people a problem.

Sniffling, I tell Mrs. Zack only that my mother is angry with me and she's locked me out. I'm too ashamed to tell her about the knife. Mrs. Zack's apartment always smells of homemade Jewish dishes, and tonight she's making potato latkes. Knowing they're one of my favorites, she quickly fixes me a plate. Sitting me in front of their new RCA color television, a luxury in 1960, she sets me up with a TV tray. I get to watch my *Woody Woodpecker Show* in color for the first time ever. The red of Woody's head is so warmly radiant and his misadventures so humorous that I temporarily forget my own drama.

Off and on I hear Mr. and Mrs. Zack whispering in their back bedroom. All I can make out is Mr. Zack saying "He has to go home," and Mrs. Zack saying "Not now, let him eat. After he's finished and she's had time to calm down, I'll walk him back." After I finish my fourth latke and the cartoon show is over, it is nearly my bedtime. Mrs. Zack takes me by the hand and escorts me through the building's quiet, carpeted inner lobby to our apartment. We stand in silence while she rings the doorbell. My mother throws open our fire-engine-red front door. Looking at Mrs. Zack in tears, Dinorah says, "I was so worried. Where was he?" Calmly, Mrs. Zack assures her that I've been with them the entire time and that she's already fed me.

Expecting my mother to fly into yet another rage, I'm relieved when Mrs. Zack says, "Jimmy, why don't you go brush your teeth and put on your pajamas for bed while your mother and I visit?" Seeing my avenue of escape, I scurry past my mother and head off to our tiny bathroom. After donning my GI Joe pajamas, I close the bedroom door, careful to leave it open just a crack. My mother and Mrs. Zack are still talking in low voices at the door as I climb in between the sheets.

The next morning, barefoot and still in my PJs, very slowly I make my way into the hallway. I smell my mother's hairspray wafting from the bathroom as I tiptoe by. She is already dressed and ready to leave for work. She's wearing a skirt like the ones on *The Donna Reed Show*. She looks so pretty when she puts on her lipstick. Sometimes she gets extra work as a model for the *Long Island Press* newspaper and magazine. She keeps a collection of her pictures in a photo album. She turns and says, "Jimmy honey, there you are. Have a good day at school today, okay? I'll see you tonight," and closes the front door behind her. I find myself confused and wondering if a punishment is in the offing for later that evening. But none will materialize, and that night she will behave like nothing happened.

2.   Locked in the Closet

MEMORIES ARE LIKE REMEMBERING snippets from a long-forgotten video montage. In this one I was in our one-bedroom apartment in Forest Hills, the one from which my father walked out on my mother and me when I was four. The building was at 111–45 Seventy-fifth Avenue just off Queens Boulevard. It was a 1940s vintage apartment building with two large black doors ringed in red and white, harkening back to a more genteel era. More recently, around the corner was a bodega where the owner was found murdered by thieves for the meager money in his cash register.

It's the apartment where I recall my first Christmas, a wonder-filled event complete with tinsel tree, resplendent with multi-colored lights—the old-fashioned, oversize kind that burnt your fingers to touch. In my video clip, it's the first Christmas after my dad left and Santa has been very, very good to me: a cowboy action figure with a companion brown horse and a full cowboy outfit for me, complete with black and white boots, hat, holster, and guns.

Our apartment was 1B. It was small with only two closets, one tiny coat closet in the living room and a second closet in the only bedroom. To my five-year-old's sense of the world, that bedroom closet was enormous, almost cavernous. It had a single light bulb high overhead on a string and the ceiling slanted downward toward the back wall. Tucked in a low corner was a Thom McAn shoebox where I stashed my collection of miniature green plastic army men. Since I couldn't reach it myself, I needed Mamí to tug on the light.

In my childhood it wasn't unusual for my mother to occasion-

An angry Dee.

ally fly into a fury, a tendency that became more pronounced after my father left. I don't recall what I'd done wrong, probably a missed homework assignment and a note home from an unhappy nun at Our Lady Queen of Martyrs. What I do remember is how my mother's countenance suddenly turned dark and threatening. She angrily ordered me into the closet for a "time-out."

"If you don't have time to do your homework, then you don't get to play either," she fumed.

I'd never had a "time-out" before. Snatching away my cowboy action figure, she shoved me toward the closet. Like many children my age, I was no great fan of the dark. On our bed's headboard sat a six-inch-tall electric Santa whose nightlight did an excellent job of dispelling my night worries. After bedtime when the bedroom door was shut and the overhead light turned off, I could hear my mother watching *Perry Mason*. The electric glow from Santa's beneficent face never failed to calm me.

In my movie clip, Mamí is roughly pushing me into the closet. She orders me to stay inside until "I say it's time to come out." As she closes the heavy white wooden closet door behind her, she reaches back and pulls the light chain. I am suddenly alone and standing in pitch darkness.

It was so black that I couldn't see my hand in front of my face. At that moment every conceivable fear rushed in, from scurrying roaches to rats with glowing red eyes to a monster so terrifying I cried out, "Mamí, Mamí please, please can I come out? Please don't leave me here! I promise I'll be good."

From the other side of the closed door her voice sounded cold and unmoved. "Don't you dare open this door or I'll beat you within an inch of your life."

From the recesses of the dark closet I continued to plead, but with no effect. I heard her leave the bedroom and then the sound of our black-and-white television turning on in the living room. My breath became shallow as I pondered how to conserve what I imagined was my limited air supply, always a concern for a severely asthmatic kid.

I imagined hearing scurrying, scratching sounds in the closet. I was desperate to escape whatever it was I imagined was moving on the floor, so I climbed onto the built-in shelves. In an act of silent defiance, I reached blindly for the light chain. Finally I grasped it, and, reasoning that she'd not see the light from the living room, I gave it a tug. The space was immediately filled with a yellow glow from the lone bulb. Looking down, I was amazed and simultaneously relieved. There were no roaches, no rats, no monsters anywhere. The heavenly aura must have scattered them back to their unseen hiding places. I climbed down and, quietly as possible, recovered my hidden stash of army men. As a distraction I arranged my army on an empty lower shelf and proceeded to conduct a silent battle of good versus evil.

After some time, I heard the television go silent. I scrambled to hide my soldiers and climbed to pull the light off. I retreated and sat in a corner just as my mother opened the door to the darkened closet. No longer furious, she sternly said, "Put on your PJs and go to bed now."

"No dinner? But I'm hungry."

"Get in bed immediately or I'll take out the belt."

I was so relieved to be free of the closet I hurriedly put on my

PJs and climbed into bed as she turned on my Santa nightlight. She headed back to the living room, closing the bedroom door behind her as she switched off the overhead light. I could hear the opening musical credits to *Bonanza* coming from the living room.

Above me on the headboard sat my aquarium with Sam, my pet turtle. And beaming down at me was Santa's jolly smile. The images of Adam, Hoss, Little Joe, and their pa, Ben Cartwright, played across my mind's eye. Even though they had lost their ma when they were still babies, I envied the Cartwright family. Their papí didn't abandon them. Their mamí never locked them in a dark closet. I fell asleep reminded that somewhere in this world there were parents with whom I could be safe.

3.   Just Dee and Me

> When the United States catches cold,
> Puerto Rico catches pneumonia.
> —BORINQUEÑO FOLK SAYING

IT WOULD TAKE YEARS OF THERAPY and a deep dive into my family's history before I'd fully grasp how I ended up locked in a closet and being chased by a knife-wielding mother. My mother's saga began in 1945, when Puerto Rico was in the midst of a catastrophic tuberculosis pandemic, the Covid of that time. With five times the U.S. mainland's rate of infection, Puerto Rico's TB outbreak was among the world's most serious then. It was an island of small proportions, only one hundred miles long by thirty-five miles wide, and the illness swept mercilessly across it. At its crest, TB killed 333 people of every 100,000 on the island, surpassing even the peak of Covid's pandemic 2020 fatalities in New York City.

My grandmother Aurea was among those infected. My fourteen-year-old mother watched terrified and helpless as her thirty-four-year-old mother slowly wasted away before her eyes. Because sanatoriums were unable to keep pace with the island's outbreak, Dinorah's father built a separate bedroom across the courtyard to quarantine my grandmother from the rest of the household. As an additional precaution, he sent my mother away to a boarding school run by Catholic nuns in the nearby town of Mayagüez. She was allowed home only on weekends and holidays.

After two years of protracted illness, my mother peered through lace curtains and glass as, in a red explosion of bloody coughing, my grandmother died. Despite her father's pleas, my mother refused to attend the funeral. For ten days she locked herself in her bedroom sobbing uncontrollably and barely eating. Her father, whom she called Papí, was powerless to console her. Eventually, Papí became frustrated and so enraged he ran away to the home of his mistress and second family across town. My mother was left in the care of a distant aunt, without a mother or a father.

Anticipating her own death and not wanting to leave my mother in the hands of Papí, my grandmother Aurea had written to her brother in New York asking him and his wife to take my mother in. They agreed, and when Aurea passed, Dinorah arranged to "visit" her godparents for a summer vacation. Initially my grandfather resisted, but he relented when her godparents assured him that she would be closely supervised and a vacation would do his grieving daughter good. But thanks to Aurea, Dinorah bravely plotted to stay in New York City and never return.

Dee, as she became known, blamed Papí's infidelity for Aurea's sickness. Once in New York, she lied about her age and landed a job as a translator at the United Nations. This became a family joke for years because when Dee took her New York high school equivalency test, the instructor, a condescending Spaniard, flunked her due to a failing class grade . . . in Spanish! Although she was a bright woman, this incident soured my mother on the idea of furthering her education.

Despite Papí's tirades and threats, Dee's resolve to stay in New York was unshakable. As a direct result she and her father did not speak for twenty-five years. While living with her godparents in their Park Slope apartment, sixteen-year-old Dee would meet a young medical student named Bernal who courted her for the next two years. Thanks to her strict upbringing by the nuns, Dee and Bernal were never left alone, nor could they even exchange a kiss.

But one evening at her godparents' apartment, Dee went alone into the kitchen to fetch dessert from the refrigerator. A visiting Bernal snuck up behind her and planted an innocent kiss on her neck. Just then her godfather and godmother, strict and devout Catholics, walked in on them. Her godparents' indignation resulted in Dee being forbidden from ever seeing the soon-to-be-doctor Bernal again. She grudgingly complied, but when she turned eighteen Dee moved out and shared an apartment in Manhattan with four other young women from Puerto Rico.

My mother described those years in Manhattan as the happiest of her life. Dee wistfully reminisced about how much fun she and her four roommates had shopping at "fancy" department stores like Gimbels and Macy's. Because one of her girlfriends knew a connected secretary at the UN named Anna Bonilla, they would often land invitations to formal dances at the Argentine embassy. Once there, they'd tango the night away with tuxedoed dignitaries and military officers in full dress uniforms. It must have been a glamourous life, like HBO's *Sex and the City*, except set in the early 1950s and without sex.

But the specter of Aurea's premature death haunted Dee. Abandoned by the loss of her mother and, then, her philandering father, and left without the affection of Bernal, her first true love, Dee made a rash decision. On the rebound from Bernal, she met and married Anna's brother, Frank "Kiko" Bonilla, who'd just returned from the Korean War. After four years of stormy marriage, Kiko would walk out on her, but not before they had their only child, me.

Many years later Dee would recount the "tragedy" of her decision to break it off with her young doctor Bernal and marry my father. "I really missed the boat with Bernal," she said. "He's now a very successful rich heart surgeon in Puerto Rico. Do you believe it? He even called me on the night of my wedding to beg me not to marry your father. What an idiot I was!"

That left just Dee and me. The name came about because one of the children of an employee couldn't pronounce Dinorah and took to calling her Dee. Soon the nickname caught on with all her friends, and me.

"I'm not one of your friends! Call me Mamí!" she'd shout.

I kept calling her Dee anyway. Unaware of it at the time, I began using Dee as a way of distancing myself from her as a parent figure. To me, she'd proven to be an unpredictable and unsafe Mamí.

4.   Our Lady Queen of Martyrs

THE FIRST DAY OF SCHOOL can be traumatic for any child, especially an only child. But for me it was downright delightful. I'd looked forward to my First Day ever since my father left us a few months earlier and my mother hired Mrs. Hirsch to do childcare. In her sixties, Mrs. Hirsch was kind but not much of a playmate. On my first day, I'd woken at dawn and was fully dressed hours before Mrs. Hirsch arrived. As Dee left for work, she turned and bent down to kiss me and whispered, "Honey, good luck at school today." The idea of spending all day in a room full of kids my own age was, for me, beyond bliss.

Our Lady Queen of Martyrs elementary school was six long blocks from our little apartment on Seventy-fifth Avenue in Forest Hills, Queens. It was all poor Mrs. Hirsch could do to keep me from running ahead to meet my new playmates. The school was an architecturally imposing building that lived up to its melodramatic name. With towering Gothic arches and columns, it was lined in dull gray and brown fieldstone and topped with a green slate roof. The nuns who ran the school dressed in the classic somber black habits common to the parochial schools of the day. My exuberance was met with equal enthusiasm by my first-grade teacher, the young and energetic Sister Ann. Under her tutelage, I jumped feet first into the full school experience, relishing the interesting lessons, new books, wonderful extracurricular activities, and, most of all, my new friends. That fall, at our first evening parent–teacher conference, a smiling Sister Ann said to my somewhat anxious mother, "Jimmy thinks school is supposed to be fun." She paused and then added with a smile, "He's a pleasure to have in class."

I volunteered for the school play that year, *The Wizard of Oz*. I played a Munchkin, and although I had only one line, I vividly recall it still: Somehow, I managed to utter my line while trying to keep my itchy fake beard from falling into my mouth. "Follow the Yellow Brick Road," I said, pointing dramatically offstage. I also signed up for Cub Scouts and took great pride in my uniform with its cool yellow bandana. Our den mother was Mrs. Luckstone, an Irish American woman with twelve children, many of whom were in our troop. On the playground, they'd join me at recess, which was my favorite half hour of the day.

I continued to love being in school, but in fourth grade my mother decided I should learn to play the piano, and the nuns offered piano lessons only during recess. For several weeks, a very patient Sister Camille gamely tried to teach me. Unfortunately, the piano was positioned next to a window that looked out directly over the playground. All I could manage to hear over the metronome keeping time was the shouts of the Luckstone kids playing tag, dodgeball, or stickball. Sister Camille eventually halted my lessons and reported to Mother Superior, "James Bonilla doesn't have the aptitude or the discipline for the piano."

That episode signaled the beginning of the end of my time at Our Lady Queen of Martyrs. Later that year, the nuns called my mother to explain that they had "diagnosed" me with a speech impediment and that I would need special remedial classes. To remedy the "disability," the nuns instructed my mother to never speak Spanish with me, as it worsened the impediment. Up to that moment I'd been functionally bilingual. Shortly after, I was transferred out of my class, away from all my friends, to a strange new classroom in the basement, classroom 1C. At recess Freddy Luckstone would tease me relentlessly, saying, "Ha! They put you in the dumb kids' class! They think you're retarded." Confused, I returned to classroom 1C only to find that all my wonderful earlier classroom experiences were supplanted by boring lessons that consisted of filling out rudimentary worksheets. Gone were the games, the fascinating classroom projects, the opportunities to interact, and the enthusiasm of Sister Ann.

In their place was the strict "no talking" harshness of Sister Badilla. One day, when I enthusiastically shouted an answer to a question posed to the class, she had a very different response from that of Sister Ann. Sister Badilla approached my desk and ordered me to put my hands palms down on the desktop. From under her billowing black robe, she suddenly withdrew a thick yardstick and swiftly cracked it over my bare knuckles. "Next time, James, maybe you'll remember to not speak unless you're called upon," she said coldly. Although stunned, I was determined to hold back tears, but that moment cemented my resolve to resist.

From then on I was the class subversive, a trait that would later serve me well as a community organizer. Unfortunately, along with my irreverent attitude, my grades also began to suffer. When Sister Badilla turned her back to the class, I'd whisper in defiance to a nearby classmate, telling a joke or complaining about her lackluster lessons. She was getting on in years and didn't hear so well, so I got away with it for a while. Unfortunately, I got more brazen and was eventually sent home with a note for my mother to sign. Always in fear of my mother's wrath, I unwisely decided to forge her signature in hopes of avoiding punishment. Since my forgery skills were not up to the task, I was easily caught. That escapade resulted in Dee having to take off a half day of work to meet with Mother Superior.

Sitting in Mother Superior's austere office, my nervous mother couldn't make eye contact. "I'm sorry, Mrs. Bonilla," Mother Superior said. "James isn't working out here. I suggest a more structured environment called Coindre Hall. It is a residential boarding school run by the Brothers of the Sacred Heart on Long Island. We believe the male presence might rein in his disobedient tendencies." My mother was raised by nuns in a convent in Puerto Rico, and her response was ingrained silent acquiescence.

And that's how I came to be kicked out of Our Lady Queen of Martyrs. I'd been one of only a handful of the school's students of color, and classroom 1C seemed to be where most of us spent our days. In adulthood, I discovered research indicating that nationally,

thousands of kids of color like me were routinely and dispropor-
tionately shunted into "special education" classrooms. One ratio-
nale given was the false belief that Latino kids either were mentally
"slow" or suffered from speech impediments. In my case I simply
had a Spanish accent. Yet in every corner of the country, not just
Queens, White teachers became convinced of our supposed mini-
mal aptitudes and need for stricter discipline. In a revealing study,
when allowed to retake IQ tests in Spanish, Mexican American students in California gained an average of 15 IQ points, enough to
test out of the "below average" range. No surprise then that in the
1960s, while Puerto Rican students constituted 20 percent of New
York City's school population, their dropout rate was between 80
and 85 percent.

The pattern of Difference = Deficit had been set in motion. Once
tracked into "special education" classes our intellectual potentials
were left to languish, thanks to the dual tyrannies of lowered expectations and systemic racism.

But at that moment, sitting with my legs dangling from the hard,
uncomfortably high oak chair in front of Mother Superior's desk,
all I could grasp was that a big change was coming. Gone would be
the long walks to school with Mrs. Hirsch, the treasured recess period with the Luckstones, and Cub Scouts. I was soon to be exiled
not just to an institution away from home but to a reform school
where New York State's court system sent kids labeled juvenile delinquents.

5.   "Lock the Doors!"

THE DAY HAD BEEN SUNNY, in the mid-eighties with a cooling breeze coming off the Atlantic, where we had spent a glorious day at Jones Beach. I'd passed the entire day bodysurfing waves that were three and four feet high. I was sunburnt and exhausted when my mom and I piled back into her car, a Corvair in "shitty yellow" (Dee's name for the pale yellow paint job). I was so spent that I didn't even begin my customary complaining about leaving the beach. Instead, I curled up on the car's back bench seat and promptly conked out. These were the days before mandatory seatbelts.

I was stirred from my nap when Dee announced, "Jimmy, time to wake up, honey. We're home." I would blame what happened next on being only half-awake. Our apartment was on the first floor of a five-story brick building in a niche just off the main lobby, next to the apartment manager's unit. Weighed down by a beach bag and picnic basket, I followed Dee into the building's inner lobby like some kind of underage porter. As an eleven-year-old, I took pride in being strong enough to serve as her packhorse. She often complimented me in front of her friends, saying "He's such a good traveling companion." I thought she just liked having a man to carry her stuff.

Approaching our red front door, she fumbled for her keys. As she slipped the key into the lock, a strange thing happened. The key turned, but the door opened only two inches. We quickly understood that the interior chain had been engaged. Puzzled, I dropped all the bags and tried to stick my eleven-year-old head in to see what was wrong. The line of sight from our front door through to the kitchen and out the narrow window was in perfect alignment. That's when I saw him: a short dark man was climbing out our kitchen window! In the fading daylight, I glimpsed his shoulders, the back of his neck, and his head before he leapt out the window onto the ground five feet below. Peering over my shoulder, my mother screamed so loudly it startled me as it echoed throughout the lobby. Desperately, she started ringing the doorbell of the apartment manager. Mr. Zack flung open his door only seconds after her first frantic ring.

I shouted, "He's gone out the window! I'm going to see if I can catch him."

To this day I don't know where that brashness came from. Mr. Zack and Dee seemed frozen in place as I tore through the lobby and headed for the alley below our kitchen window. As the building's heavy black front doors closed behind me I caught the trailing sound of Dee's voice: "Where do you think you're going? Stop! Jimmy, STOP! Come—"

The massive doors closed and I was cut off from hearing the rest. Running at full steam, I rounded the building and then slowed to peek around the corner in the hopes of spotting the intruder. I'm not sure what I thought I'd do but later I explained, "Maybe I could've gotten his license plate like they do on TV."

Fortunately, for me, the alley was deserted. *Where did he go? How did he get away so fast?* Just then Dee came up behind me and, grabbing me by my T-shirt, dragged me back into the building. Reentering the lobby, we saw Mr. Zack had fetched his bolt cutters. It seemed to take forever, but eventually he managed to snap the stubborn chain. Meanwhile, Mrs. Zack had called the NYPD to report a burglary in progress. Although we finally had access, Dee refused to step into the apartment. She was sobbing deeply as we waited for a patrol car to make its appearance. Mrs. Zack took my mother into their apartment to wait. I took it as my solemn duty to wait outside by the front door of the building for the police. Like many sons, I hated being around my mother when she cried.

Thirty-five minutes later, two uniformed officers in a black,

At Jones Beach with Dee.

white, and green patrol car pulled up in front of the building. I ran toward them waving my arms. "It's here! The robbery is here." Unhurried, they put on their hats and slowly followed me into the building. I recall thinking *On TV the police always come running.* In hindsight, these two had probably figured out our perp was long gone. As soon as they appeared at the Zacks' door my mother began crying uncontrollably. Hiccupping between sobs, she said, "I won't go in there. I . . . I . . . can't," she stammered as she blew her nose.

"We'll check it out," said the older of the two cops. He was at least six feet four inches, with salt-and-pepper hair showing under his patrol cap.

"Can I come, can I come too?" I pleaded.

The second cop, shorter, younger, with red hair and a ruddy complexion, said, "Nah, kid. You stay here and keep your mom safe."

After a while they returned and the bigger cop announced, "It's all clear, Mrs. Bonilla. Nothing looks broken or jimmied. Does anyone else have a key that you know of?"

In a low voice my mother said, "Just my ex, and he abandoned us years ago." Then her eyes darted in the direction of Mrs. Zack.

"Maybe you should look around while we're here and see if anything's missing," suggested Officer Red Hair.

Eyes wide, Dee inched into our apartment with one officer on each side of her while I was ordered to wait in the Zacks' apartment. She clutched the arm of the bigger officer, her face ashen. In less than three minutes, I heard my mother yelling through the wall, "It's gone! My wedding ring is gone!" Racing in, I saw the two uniforms exchange knowing glances. Relieved to find that no harm had come to my pet turtle, Sam, I began an inventory to check if any of my toys were missing. Dee collapsed on our bed, weeping loudly while Mrs. Zack gently put her arm around her heaving shoulders.

"Not much more we can do here tonight," said Officer Red Hair. "I'll leave the card of our burglary division on the kitchen table." Both officers seemed relieved to leave the scene.

For the next three nights we stayed with one of Dee's work friends. In the meantime, Mr. Zack changed the locks. Dee agreed to return only after her boss at the Long Island Press, Harris Sr., and his eldest son, Harris Jr., agreed to rotate shifts sleeping on our living room couch. Harris Jr. came equipped for his shift with a Louisville Slugger. The sight of him, an amateur weightlifter who stood six foot two, would be sufficient to scare off any returning thieves.

Weeks and months passed while my mother struggled to put the robbery behind her. I was reassured by the procession of beefy men from Dee's job sleeping on our couch, but Dee's crying jags persisted. For the rest of the summer, she made a ritual of insisting a man enter our apartment before she felt safe to go inside.

The combination of my mother's already anxious disposition and the trauma of the break-in finally got the better of her. With little explanation, one weekend early in September I was deposited at the home of "Aunt Lee" and "Uncle Charlie" with a suitcase and my shoebox full of toy green army men. We weren't actually related; Lee worked for my mother at the Long Island Press and lived in Queens Village. Dee told me she was going to visit her sick aunt in Puerto Rico for a while. Lee and Charlie always treated me like an adopted grandchild. Best of all, they had two teenagers who played with me when they weren't at school.

First one week passed and then two. After the second week

I began asking after Dee. Aunt Lee gently said, "Oh sweetie, she's away resting at a kind of camp for adults. When she feels less fearful she'll be back to bring you home." That was Aunt Lee's kind way of saying my mother had been hospitalized with a "nervous breakdown." Meanwhile, I felt like I was on an extended vacation. I had two teenagers serving as my doting big brother and big sister and their two playful poodles to distract me. Although I suffered from severe allergies to dogs and cats that normally triggered my asthma attacks, Aunt Lee's poodles were dander-free.

Midway through the third week a more visibly relaxed Dee appeared at the door at suppertime. She was wearing a blue and white polka-dot dress and announced she was there to collect me and my new GI Joe, courtesy of Uncle Charlie.

After returning to our Forest Hills apartment, Dee never again spoke about my aunt in Puerto Rico or where she'd been. I somehow knew not to ask. But within the month, we moved to a new garden apartment in Queens Village. She was adamant that this one be located on the second floor. To this day I still sleep with a Louisville Slugger by my bed.

On our frequent rides into Jamaica from Queens Village, Dee would point out the windshield and say, "Those people would just as soon cut your throat as look at you." The idea that a White parent from an overwhelmingly White suburban area would instruct their children to lock the car doors as they cruise through unfamiliar Black and Latino neighborhoods is disappointing but not especially surprising. What was confusing was that my mother was Puerto Rican. For my twelve-year-old self, the cognitive dissonance created by her simple directive was a cause for irony, uncomfortable laughter, and sadness.

If only I'd had the impudence back then to point out, "But we're Puerto Rican. Aren't we 'those' people?" Maybe that's why we never lived in Black or Puerto Rican neighborhoods in my youth. My mother would suffer a longer commute in exchange for being safely ensconced in a predominately White middle- or working-class area in Queens. Since I couldn't play stickball (the ball was too fast and small for me to see), I'd always find a few kids, including kids of color, on the street for a pickup touch football game. The larger ball was one I could see. But the neighborhoods were invariably and historically White. Forest Hills, where we'd lived for many years, was at the time a Jewish enclave.

Eventually we moved from Queens Village, an Italian American community, to Richmond Hill, a strictly working-class White neighborhood. But even Dee's efforts at making us safe couldn't escape the crime waves that engulfed New York in the late 1960s and early 1970s. We lived through one of the city's most violent eras. Even venerable Forest Hills, home to the Arthur Ashe Stadium, didn't escape the times.

While we lived at Seventy-fifth Avenue in Forest Hills, the owner of our corner bodega was found shot dead in his store. I vividly remember the bright yellow police tape partially obscuring my eight-year-old's view of the black body bag being carried on a gurney as onlookers stared in silence.

Then there was the robbery of our little first-floor apartment. The one thing missing was the rather expensive wedding ring from my father. Unleashing her wrath at my father's memory, Dee conjectured, "I'd not put it past your father that he hired a man to steal back that ring. It was the only thing stolen."

It was undeniable that my father had a long memory and was one to hold a grudge. On one of my monthly weekend visitations to his and my grandmother's apartment in Flushing, he pulled into the underground parking lot only to find someone had parked in his reserved space. He positioned me by the elevator, instructing me to whistle if somebody started coming down. He then let the air out of the violator's tires—all four. Standing watch, I hoped no one would come down. My dried-out lips would have been incapable of puckering up enough for a whistle. After my mother's accusation and with the memory of my father's "get even" nature, I simply kept silent. I intuited this was a battle I would be wise not to get caught up in. Given the precarious state of my sense of family, even as a child I knew picking sides would clearly be a lose–lose proposition for me.

6. Doña Luisa, Mi Nana

MY MOTHER DISLIKED my father's mother, Doña Luisa, but reluctantly respected and feared her powers. Nana was an espirituista, a Puerto Rican healer. One scorching mid-August afternoon, after falling asleep on a Long Island beach, my mother woke to second-degree burns over much of her exposed fair-skinned body. Returning to their apartment in great pain, Nana cut her out of the bathing suit and forced my mother to spend the night in a bathtub of water, sprinkled with herbs and healing ointments. To my mother's shock, when she woke up the next morning, she climbed out of the tub without so much as a blister or peel on her body.

A further sign of Nana's gift as a healer was how she successfully treated my frequent asthma attacks. She'd make a special concoction of coffee and herbs and have me drink it down. Decades later, modern medicine would "discover" caffeine to be one of the more effective treatments for youthful asthma sufferers.

As a teenager, I was perplexed by my mother's hostility toward Nana. One night, eating ice cream over pound cake covered in chocolate syrup at our small Formica kitchen table, I ventured to ask, "Dee, tell me about Nana." Ice cream always put my mother in a relaxed mood: "self-medicating with food," my therapist would later say when I described a similar pattern in myself.

Lighting a cigarette from a burner on our stovetop, Dee said, "No one dared call her 'Grandma.' Everyone addressed her either as Nana or Doña Luisa."

Up to her death, Nana refused to speak English. She was that proud of her Puerto Rican lineage. In fact, because my mother wouldn't speak Spanish to me (under strict orders from the nuns at Our Lady Queen of Martyrs), the only Spanish I consistently heard growing up was in Nana's home.

Despite being only four foot eleven inches tall, Nana quietly commanded the respeto that came with the title Doña, an honorific among Latinos reserved for elders. Before Nana's forebearers came to Puerto Rico in the 1870s, they had run a successful food import–export business in Corsica. In Puerto Rico Nana ran that business, and as a result her family was comfortably well off. Although her business acumen served the family well, her husband Don Berna-dino's photography studio in Mayagüez often struggled. Mayagüez is one of the larger metropolises on the island, located on the western shore facing the Caribbean Sea. His involvement in the turbulent politics of Puerto Rico and his support of the fiery Independista Pedro Albizu Campos cost him many customers.

Death threats aimed at Don Bernadino because of his politics forced Nana and the family to flee north to New York City. In the 1940s and 1950s, they joined the waves of Puerto Ricans who

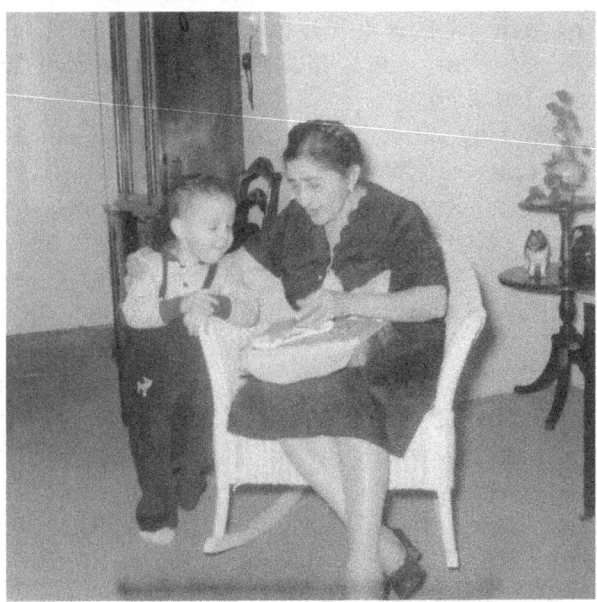

With my Nana in 1957.

boarded ships like the Marine Tiger to escape the grinding poverty and political unrest seizing the island.

Nana's brother lived in Spanish Harlem, where they stayed for their first two months in Manhattan. Nana eventually used the profits from the sale of her import–export business to buy a modest brick duplex in Jamaica, Queens.

"Your father's mother was a very savvy businesswoman. She insisted on a duplex because it had a rental apartment in the basement," my mother recalled. "Your father once told me how Nana fought with Don Bernadino about the decision to buy the place. When he told me that, I was shocked. Your Nana was usually such a quiet woman. But Nana put her foot down and they bought the place in 1952. Within a year of their moving in, Don Bernadino had dropped dead."

Tipping her cigarette ashes into her empty coffee cup, my mother continued, "Imagine . . . if your Nana hadn't stood up to him."

After Don Bernadino's death, with my father fighting in Korea, Doña Luisa was left to raise three girls by herself. Dee explained how the rental income kept Nana's family from losing their home on 169th Street. My mother and father spent my first four years living in that downstairs apartment. Dee added, her face puckering as if she sucked a sourball, "That woman even charged us rent while we lived there."

Pausing to take a drag on her cigarette, Dee began to relive another memory. "When I was pregnant with you, your Nana insisted I go to her doctor, a very old, very cold German man. I told him that under no circumstances did I wish to suffer during childbirth. He promised he'd see to it that I be given sedatives to dull the pain. But the day I went into labor, he was nowhere to be found." Dee's face darkened. "The nurses wouldn't give me anything, not even an aspirin for the pain. I suffered through labor like a wild animal forced to give birth in a barn. It was horrible!"

Suppressing a grimace, I thought, *Geez, what child likes to hear how resentful their mother is of the "horrible" experience of their birth?* Later I read that it isn't unusual for mothers who didn't have a mother themselves to develop resentment toward their own children for having the mother they never had.

From left: Uncle Ernesto, Nana, Titi Anna, Titi Judy, Dee, my father Kiko, and an unknown woman.

Pouring more Bosco over a fresh scoop of vanilla ice cream, Dee continued, "I'll always blame your nana for forcing me to see that quack." Even after all those years, Dee still held the grudge—and decades after her experience, new data reports reveal that systemic mistreatment of women of color by the overwhelmingly White medical establishment still persists.

As she momentarily withdrew from her venom to take a spoonful of ice cream, I recalled an image of playing stoopball on the steps of Nana's duplex in Jamaica. As I played by myself, I would hear the rumblings of the elevated J and Z trains. I fondly pictured Nana keeping a watchful eye from the comfort of her white wicker rocker as she crocheted on the screened-in porch. Her long gray hair, which she religiously combed one hundred times each night before bed, was braided into a tight bun on the top of her head. Nana kept a light blue and gold perfume bottle of eau de cologne on her bedside table next to her silver brush. I associate its orange and peach scent with her to this day.

Dee interrupted my reverie. "That woman charged us for your child care, her only grandchild!" she said, crushing out her cigarette.

After my parents' divorce, Nana ceased to provide after-school child care while I went to Our Lady Queen of Martyrs. But thanks to her insistence, I got to visit her and my absentee father on holidays, and on those visits I soaked up her and my Titi Anna's unconditional love.

7.　My First Bike

I WAS AS EXCITED AND EAGER as only a seven-year-old can be. It was the day after Christmas and my father was coming over to bring me my belated Christmas present. He had told me to wait outside our building as he had "something big" to unload from his trunk. He promised to be there at 1:00 p.m.

Since my parents had separated two years earlier, his visits had been sporadic, at best. I was in front of our building at 12:45, joined by my stickball pals Jimmy and Johnny Lee, the Chinese American sons of the owners of our local laundry on Queens Boulevard. Intrigued by the idea of a big surprise, the Lee brothers and our friend Peter hung out to see what was what.

As usual, Dad was late, and at 1:35 I had to pee like a racehorse. I asked Jimmy if he'd be willing to keep an eye out in case my dad showed up while I ran back inside to relieve myself.

"Yeah sure," Jimmy said, "but I don't know what your dad looks like."

I had to think about it for a minute. "He kinda looks like that man in *To Kill a Mockingbird,* I think his name is Gregory Peck. Except my dad is shorter and has black eyeglasses. He doesn't wear a coat, but wears these starchy white shirts and brown slacks." Dad's olive complexion and black wavy hair stood in sharp contrast to his white Arrow dress shirts. A former semipro baseball player, he moved smoothly and easily in his body. "Oh yeah, he chain-smokes Camel cigarettes and drives a black Caddy with those cool red fins in back." I didn't add that Dad always smelled of Old Spice after-shave, a telltale sign of his masculinity that I couldn't wait to emulate as soon as I was old enough to shave.

I returned quickly, and by now a small crowd of local kids had gathered to see what the fuss was about. Shortly before 2:00 p.m. Dad's Caddy turned off Queens Boulevard and ever so slowly glided down Seventy-fifth Avenue, where he double-parked in front of our building. As he opened the driver's side door his face registered surprise at the welcoming gaggle of young boys. They'd heard me bragging about his exploits teaching baseball in Japan in the 1940s and 1950s, so they pressed in close to meet the famous Frank "Kiko" Bonilla. Not many celebrities visited our neighborhood.

Good-naturedly, he tussled my hair and that of Jimmy and Johnny and proceeded to the rear of the car, carefully making his way through the throng. Prolonging the drama, he pretended to fumble with the keys until I begged, "Come on, Papí—open it. Open it!"

"Okay, okay, just keep this motley crew back," he said, grinning.

As the huge trunk lid slowly popped open, I immediately spied chrome handlebars and a single bike tire standing on end. In one smooth move, Dad hoisted the bike up and out of the trunk and onto the nearby sidewalk. I was so excited I hopped up and down, saying, "My first bike, oh boy, oh boy!" It was the same metallic green as Steve McQueen's Ford Mustang in the movie *Bullitt*. The handlebars had red grips with white streamers coming out the ends. He positioned the kickstand as I slowly circled the bike and took it all in. Since the white training wheels were already installed, my dad asked, "Want to try it out?"

The snow had melted into dirty brown piles and the sidewalks were mostly clean and dry. Hesitantly, I climbed on, aware that all my friends were watching and that I didn't want to look as afraid as I felt. I'd never ridden before, so Dad positioned himself to support me. One of his gloved hands was on the handlebar to help me steer while the other gripped the back of the seat to steady me. Wobbling at first, with him running alongside, I slowly gathered confidence and momentum. After a few minutes, I turned to tell him how fun this was when I saw he was trotting alongside me but had already let go. Surprised, I shouted, "I'm doing it! I'm doing it myself!" For a split second I dared lift my right hand from the handle grip to ring the bike's bell. In the background I could hear my chums whooping and cheering me on.

Ten days later it was my birthday and my mother gave me a red bicycle with training wheels. Confused, I asked, "But I already have a bike. What am I going to do with this one?" I felt devastated and afraid to tell Nana and Papí.

"Oh, that's fine," she replied. "You can keep the green one at your Nana's place to ride when you're there."

Too late! I don't think she knew that I'd already developed a strong attachment to Bullitt, the green bike. I didn't want to antagonize her, so I kept my mouth shut, but my stomach churned. Mysteriously, before I could bring Bullitt to Nana's, it was stolen from a locked storage room in our building's basement. Dee could be spiteful, and she was the only one with the key to our storage unit. Once again the seven-year-old me was a mediator trying to keep my parents' mutual antagonism at bay. The child version of me felt overwhelmed and alone.

8. Coindre Hall

T HE FOG FROM LONG ISLAND SOUND clung stubbornly to the tops of the white pine trees as we drove up the half-mile road marked PRIVATE. I was sitting in the backseat of Harris Sr.'s 1963 Ford Galaxie. He was my mom's boss, platonic beau, and, I later suspected, financial backer. His brand-new moss-green Galaxie still had that showroom car smell. I was being delivered to Coindre Hall, a private reform boarding school on a remote peninsula in Huntington Station, New York. As we approached the driveway, a huge castle loomed into view. The slate roofs were the color of congealed blood. Shades of Harry Potter's Hogwarts, except without the welcoming upper classmates or kindly Professor Dumbledore.

What I'd done to deserve being expelled from my fourth-grade Catholic school class wasn't entirely a mystery. But to my nine-year-old mind, it seemed minuscule in comparison to the enormity of being banished by my mother from our tiny apartment and my friends in Forest Hills. I had tried every trick I could conjure: crying, pleading for forgiveness, promising to be good. Nothing had worked.

As we turned into the circular drive of the castle that was Coindre Hall, it finally loomed into full view. Its battlements and five-story turrets pierced the gray sky. Hesitantly, I stepped out on the crusty gravel and gazed at the imposing granite stairs that led to the front entrance of the school, my new home away from home. In front of a pair of enormous dark wooden doors crisscrossed with brass bolts awaited Brother Arnold. My mother raced up the steps

Coindre Hall in 1963.

ahead of her boss and me and began crying on the brother's chest. He was tall and lanky in his black cassock and white collar and seemed unfazed by her outburst. With a practiced hug he consoled her, assuring her that I'd be in good hands. Although he was not that old a man, when he bent down I glimpsed his thinning black hair and large, shiny, pale forehead. While my mother wiped her tears and blew her nose on his proffered white handkerchief, he stepped forward and met me near the top step. He shook my hand tightly. Not a particularly intuitive child, even I could ascertain that rough hand's silent message: "There'll be no crying here, young man." So I didn't cry.

After showing us to my cot in the fifth graders' dormitory and depositing my lone bag, he took us outside to show us the grounds. I was relieved to be out from the castle's dark, walnut-paneled, claustrophobia-inducing hallways. Coindre Hall was built copying the style of a French chateau by a wealthy Huntington pharmaceutical tycoon.

My first week was a mix of early-morning masses, silent assemblies, demanding classes, and the much-anticipated recess hour. I especially enjoyed the soccer fields, not because I was good at soccer but because of their sweeping panoramic views of Oyster Bay. The salty scent of the ocean air became a needed balm for my homesick soul.

The school's property ran down a long sprawling hill to a two-story boathouse on the water's edge. It once housed the family's sixty-foot yacht. The older boys relished telling us that not only was the boathouse haunted but it was sometimes used as a detention center for classmates caught breaking the brothers' strict code of conduct. The Brothers of the Sacred Heart took in juvenile delinquents from New York's family court system for a hefty fee. Unfortunately, these mostly Brown and Black kids suffered a disproportionate share of evening visitations to the boathouse. Because it was situated at least 1,500 feet from the main mansion, we never heard their cries of pain, but returnees would sometimes drop their uniform trousers to reveal the bloody welts from Brother Arnold's paddle. A few would return with black eyes and blue and purple bruises on their cheeks and arms. We lived in dread of hearing the command "Mr. So-and-So, assume the position," the prelude to a butt whipping.

One day, standing at the back of a long line waiting for our daily chapel service, I heard a commotion from the front. It was a hall rule that absolute silence be maintained at all times during chapel. I could hear Brother Arnold thundering, "Quiet means quiet!" This was followed by a volley of heavy slaps and then low whimpering. Listening intently, the boys around me strained to see. Brother Arnold came barreling around the corner, roughly shoving our classmate Bailey ahead of him. Brother Arnold's face was dark and pinched with rage. Bailey's white shirt was no longer tucked into his pants and his face was swollen and red, his right eye half shut. His gaze turned downward as he used the sleeve of his navy-blue uniform jacket to wipe the bloody snot leaking from his nose. Already a fragile kid, Bailey hiccupped, trying desperately to stifle his sobs. At only nine years of age, even though I'd never heard the term "child abuse," I knew enough to sense that what had been done to Bailey was wrong.

The next several days and nights passed uneventfully but always concluded with my quietly crying myself to sleep. The brothers took turns doing "night patrol" in the dorms, which was how I first met the kindly Brother Leonard. At seventy-five, he was the eldest of the order and also the school's nurse. Weeping in my bed well after lights out with my head under the covers, one night I heard a soft voice nearby whisper, "Crying is nothing to be ashamed of. Even the bigger boys here cry from time to time. I tell them not to feel lonely. Jesus is looking out for you." Slowly I pulled the sheet down to my chin. Because he was holding a flashlight by his side I could only make out Brother Leonard's distinctly stooped silhouette. Suddenly his arm disappeared into his cassock pocket. Fearing a slap, I held my breath. He withdrew it slowly and, shining in his flashlight, I saw he was holding a black rosary with a tiny silver cross. He placed it gently in my hand and then, without a word, proceeded with his assigned bed checks. As his flashlight disappeared from view, I was left alone in the dark again. I ran my tear-stained fingertips along the smooth wooden beads and promptly fell asleep.

There would be more dark nights and days at Coindre Hall, including my own run-in with Brother Arnold, but that night I had found a friend and future mentor. Brother Leonard's confidence in my intellect would slowly undo some of the beliefs I had internalized about not being very smart.

9. Sammy, My Beagle

THERE CAN BE NO GREATER COMPANION for an only child of nine than a pet, especially a dog. When my parents were first married we lived in my grandmother's basement apartment in Astoria, Queens. My father had a dog named Red, and I'm told that Red adored me. I have pictures of Red letting me pull his ears and lie on top of him when I was no older than two. Unfortunately, I was then first diagnosed as having an allergy to animals that, with prolonged exposure, resulted in asthma attacks. These spells caused some of my first visits to the emergency room.

After my father left my mother and after the robbery at our Forest Hills apartment, my mom and I moved to Queens Village and the second-story apartment. In the fall of 1963 I began spending my weeks sleeping away from home at Coindre Hall, and during one of those first weekends back home my mother surprised me. Waiting excitedly at our front door was a beagle puppy named Sam. He was cute, as all puppies are, with big floppy ears and brown and white markings, but he also stood apart. Sam had a pink nose!

Sam and I bonded immediately. One of our favorite games was racing each other around our one-bedroom U-shaped apartment. Beginning in the bedroom, we'd race to the first turn by the front door and then cut hard right toward the dining room. Then there'd be another hard right turn into the living room, completing the U. At the far wall of our living room was our electric faux fireplace, where we'd turn around and reverse course and race back to the bedroom.

Sam was smart, and once he got the hang of the game he began to beat me regularly. One obstacle, however, kept me competitive. Keeping with my mother's decorating theme of early Americana, at the top of the turn by the front door she placed a small oval braided rug. Sam was a hunting dog, and his boundless enthusiasm coupled with his speed resulted in his taking the turn by the front door way too fast. As he careened around the turn trying to get his footing, the braided rug would slide with his weight and the rug and Sam would slam into the front door. While he'd be shaking it off, the crash afforded me my break and I'd seize the lead. No matter how many times we'd race the course, Sam continued to slide on the rug and only be stopped when he slammed into the door. After a few rounds, I began to understand that Sam didn't care about beating me—he was enjoying his thrill ride on the sliding rug. Whenever

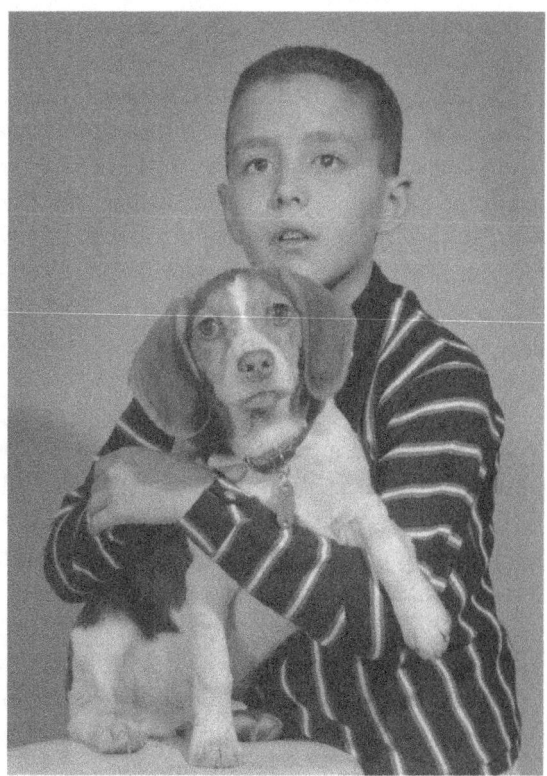

With my dog Sam.

he'd get excited (like by a visitor to the apartment), he'd race around until he slammed into the door.

My romance with Sam was short-lived. My allergies to dogs ultimately escalated into more frequent and serious asthma attacks on weekends, leading to Friday and Saturday middle-of-the-night trips to the emergency room. Because of the robbery I knew Dee hated living alone and that once I went away to boarding school she was on her own. But I was well into my teens before I understood that she had gotten Sam primarily as company and protection for herself and only secondarily to atone for sending me away to Coindre Hall. One snowy Friday in January I came home from the train station looking forward to playing with Sam, but after opening the front door all I found waiting was an empty apartment. No Sam.

My mother said, "Jimmy, we have to discuss something." She sat me down at the dining room table. "Because Sam was making you sick I had to arrange for him to go live with a nice family on a farm in Connecticut."

I didn't know then that "the farm" was an age-old euphemism employed by parents. I had intuited my time with Sam would be short-lived because of my asthma, but as I sat in the dining room gazing at the braided oval rug that had been Sam's thrill ride I couldn't keep my lower lip from trembling. Not wanting to seem a crybaby, I pushed back my tears. That night I dreamt of Sam romping in a field with his new owners, a brother and sister roughly my age. In the morning I could feel the dampness on my pillowcase where my tears had fallen.

Had I discovered Sam's true whereabouts, I doubt that my grief could have been any greater. Years later my mother confessed what really happened: like many dogs purchased from "puppy mills," Sam hadn't received all his shots, and only a few short months after coming home to us he developed canine distemper, a frequently fatal disease.

As my mother was confessing, she sobbed, "We did the merciful thing so that the poor thing didn't have to suffer." At the time I wondered, *So you didn't send him away to spare me the asthma attacks?* Once again her tears took precedence over my feelings, and I found myself consoling her.

I speculated that it was the depth of my mother's fear of being alone and being abandoned—first by her mother, then her father, boyfriend, husband, and now me—that eventually drove her to get a dog. In the end, even Sam abandoned her. Yet the weight of my mother's fears wouldn't fully manifest for another six years. And when they did, they'd slam into me like a runaway subway train.

10. "Hey, Spic!"

THE YEAR 1964 WAS A TUMULTUOUS ONE. The Beatles had taken America by storm singing "I Want to Hold Your Hand." As the country was gripped by racial civil unrest, Bob Dylan sang "The Times They Are a-Changin'," and I was about to lose most of the vision in my one good eye.

On a wet Monday afternoon that March, it was so raw outside that our recess was relocated to Coindre Hall's basement recreation hall. It was a dark walnut-paneled room with low ceilings that housed two pool tables, a knock-hockey board, and a Ping-Pong table. The adjoining locker room consisted of a row of tan lockers and stairs that led to classrooms above. Brother Arnold sometimes used its long bench to mete out corporeal punishment. His infamous tagline was "Mr. X, assume the position." That meant the student about to receive whacks from his wooden paddle must bend over with his hands on the bench.

Sean Ryan and I were playing a very competitive game of horseshoes and he was losing, badly. Sean was never a good loser. One of his errant horseshoe tosses rolled into the locker room next door and I chased after it, crouching down to search in the dark recesses under the stairs for the red rubber horseshoe. The light under the stairs was dim and I was having no luck. Meanwhile, unbeknownst to me, Sean had already found the ring after it rolled out from underneath the stairs.

After several moments searching, I stepped out of the gloom of the stairwell and heard Sean's high-pitched voice hiss, "Hey, spic—catch!"

Blinking at his use of the word, I slowly turned to face him. He then whipped the horseshoe at me full force. Since my eyes were still adjusting to the glare of the bright room, I had no time to put up my hands to protect myself. Thanks to my congenital cataracts, I'd already lost the sight in my left eye. The horseshoe hit me square in my right eye. The pain was unlike anything I had experienced before. It felt like a hot spike had been driven into my eye socket. I saw bright bursts of light so intense that they obscured the room from my view. The pain was excruciating and I was immediately nauseous. I stumbled blindly into the rec room, clutching at a pool table's edge for balance. Unable to keep my legs under me, I lowered myself onto the soft green felt and momentarily passed out.

When I awoke moments later I was in agony and cognizant that I couldn't see much beside distorted halos of colored lights. Not sure if help had been summoned, I cried out, "Help, I can't see! I can't see!"

I heard Sean's voice nearby saying "He's faking, he's all right," but the hesitancy in his voice betrayed both uncertainty and concern. I was so dizzy I couldn't raise my head for fear of throwing up. Suddenly a large face loomed into view inches from my own.

Brother Arnold demanded, "What happened here?"

One of the older boys said, "I think he got hit in the face by a horseshoe." I must have lost consciousness again. The next thing I recall is waking up in the school infirmary.

I heard Brother Leonard's kindly voice saying, "Good, you're awake. You took quite a blow there." His voice was full of concern as he explained my good right eye was quite bloodshot. "I'm going to wrap both eyes to minimize any unnecessary movement," he said as he carefully placed pads, then a gauze bandage, around my head. He lightly positioned an icepack over the bandages, and after a while the sharp pain diminished to just a terrible ache. Once Brother Leonard was done wrapping the gauze over both my eyes I was completely without sight. Besides the softness of his voice, all I could hear was the television coverage of New York's Saint Patrick's

Day parade. The sounds of the bagpipes and drums became a welcome distraction.

For the next three days, I was the lone occupant of the infirmary. I spent my days and nights listening to television and chatting with Brother Leonard. My only visitors were Brother Arnold and, later, Bailey, who came every day to receive his asthma medication. He was a fellow "wheezer," like me.

In a whisper Bailey told me, "Brother Arnold really laid his paddle into Sean." Having seen the wrath of Brother Arnold, I'm sure I felt some compassion for Sean. But what I said to Bailey was "Good. I hope he can't sit down for a month."

Friday was the day most boys went home for the weekend to be with their families. All except the boys who were custodial wards of the state—they stayed. In a departure from routine, Brother Arnold accompanied me on the bus ride to Long Island's Huntington train station. Because my eyes were still heavily bandaged, he even sat beside me in the railroad car. It was a long, quiet, awkward trip. We finally arrived at the end of the line: Jamaica, Queens. Abruptly, Brother Arnold took my arm and led me off the train onto the platform. My mother was waiting, and by her voice I could tell she was clearly distressed to see my eyes covered in gauze.

Brother Arnold's voice, ever full of authority, explained, "Oh, Jimmy had a little accident. We've been applying ice twice a day to the area, and the swelling has gone down. I'm sure he'll be able to rejoin us on Sunday." My mother politely thanked him and took me by the arm and briskly walked me along the platform.

"We're going to see Dr. Pearly," she whispered, clutching my arm as we awkwardly made our way down a set of stairs toward the cabstand. "When I called him about your accident he agreed to keep the office open until we arrive. That man is a saint." I was uncomfortable about the fuss and felt anxious about the cost of the cab ride from Queens to Dr. Pearly's Midtown Manhattan office.

"It's no big deal. It doesn't even hurt anymore," I protested. That wasn't quite true. It still felt like I'd gotten punched in the face.

"It's your one good eye and we're not taking any chances," my mother said definitively.

Forty-five minutes later I was sitting in Dr. Pearly's office with my chin on the cup of his exam chair. The brightness of the beam of light from his machine, in contrast to the darkness of the exam room, pained my eye. His manner, usually light and friendly on our annual visits, was deadly serious.

In his soft voice he told my mother, "Dinorah, I'm having him admitted to Manhattan Eye and Ear Hospital tonight. I don't like what I'm seeing. There's been substantial internal bleeding and I'm not sure it's stopped."

I suddenly felt lightheaded, but this time I managed to stay vertical. I spent the next week in the hospital, during which a surgeon operated to stem the internal hemorrhaging in my right eye. I returned to Coindre Hall ten days after the accident, but my vision was drastically reduced. Due to the internal bleeding the cataract in my right eye was now twice as thick. I was no longer able to read regular print without a magnifier and I had to rely on Brother Leonard's help for my schoolwork. I finished out the year and at the end of May went home for summer recess.

The vision in my good eye had been dramatically reduced to 20/800. I was now officially considered legally blind, which meant that I required the kind of special education services that were only offered in New York City's public school system. I'd never see Brother Leonard, Brother Arnold, Bailey, or Sean at Coindre Hall again. In September my mother enrolled me in the bizarrely named "Sight Conservation" class at PS 127 in Queens. My life as a blind person had begun.

11.   "Sight Conservation"

BECAUSE OF MY LOSS OF SIGHT at Coindre Hall, I needed remedial help in school. Many sighted people believe that if
you're "blind," you must live in total darkness. I wasn't totally blind,
but blind enough to make reading books or the blackboard, or seeing to drive, impossible. I was now not simply visually impaired, as
I had been before, but legally blind—or, not to put too fine a point
on it, blind.

Neither Coindre Hall nor the Catholic school system in New
York at the time saw the need to assist "special needs" students like
me. As a result, I was referred to the public schools, specifically Van
Wyck Junior High School (PS 217) in Queens, which supposedly had
designated programs for kids with visual impairments. Weirdly,
they were called "Sight Conservation" classes. Besides attending
regular classes, where I was given seating near the blackboard and
additional time on tests (retyped in large print), I was tracked into
typing classes. I hated typing, preferring to have my mother, the
professional secretary, type my papers. Perhaps their thought was
"At least let's give the blind kid something he can do to stay off welfare." Whether out of hubris or defiance, I nearly failed typing.

I soon recognized that academics were not a priority at PS 217.
Survival was. Classes were overcrowded and the teaching was unremarkable. Fights on the playground and in the cafeteria were a
daily occurrence. In an effort to desegregate schools, the Board of
Education bused kids of color from less affluent neighborhoods
like South Jamaica to schools in well-off, predominantly White

communities. An unintended consequence of the all-White board's decision was that groups of Black and Latino youth were set up to see one another as interlopers and antagonists. Between 1967 and 1969, schools like Van Wyck were the frequent site of conflicts that pitted Black, White, and Latino students against one another.

Because I was bused separately in a small van with other kids with disabilities, dubbed the "Gimp Bus," a pair of older kids quickly identified me as easy pickings. My first week at PS 217 I ran into the two South Jamaica boys as I was getting off the bus. Strolling confidently up to me, they demanded I hand over my lunch money. Because they'd already picked on Carlos, another blind kid on my van, they thought I'd forfeit my money with no fuss. Standing nearly a head taller than me, one shoved me into the entrance hallway doors and waited for me to empty my pockets. Intuiting that this would be the beginning of a pattern of intimidation, I hesitated. Since the Forest Hills robbery, I'd taken to working out regularly with heavy weights. At that moment, I reasoned that even if I got beat, I was strong enough to get in some good licks that might persuade them to not target me again. Putting down my book bag, I raised my fists. Surprised at this show of bravado, by a blind kid no less, they paused, then laughed.

"Motherfucker, we going to jack you up," the taller one snarled. Suddenly, from my right I heard an unfamiliar voice say, "Not today, pendejos." Turning, I saw two students, not much bigger than me, walking toward my two tormentors. I didn't see faces well and had no idea who they were, but their Nuyorican accents were revealing.

Surprised by this turn of events, the shorter of the two kids said, "Ahhh, Monaco, we just messin' with him, being the new kid and all. We weren't goin' to hurt him any."

As quickly as the two South Jamaica boys had appeared, they melted into the steady stream of students filing into the school as the first bell rang. Shaking ever so slightly, I picked up my bag and hoisted it back on my shoulder. The younger of my two rescuers stretched out his hand. "My name is Monaco Baez. This is my older brother, Chicky."

Because I was legally blind, I was eligible to get Monaco assigned to show me where my classes were. I soon learned that he and his two brothers were legendary at the school for both their uncanny strength and their fighting prowess. Juan, the third and oldest brother, had gone to PS 217 and gone on to fight semipro at the Golden Gloves championships at Madison Square Garden—before, it was rumored, he got sent upstate to Attica state penitentiary. The Baez brothers never started a fight, but the tough kids at 217 learned the hard way they were always the ones left standing at the end of one. No one messed with them. It seemed the Fates had found me a bodyguard.

My time at PS 217 was unremarkable, except for the daily threat of violence, and learning how to box from Monaco. His lesson was short and to the point. "Since you can't see shit, you won't see most punches coming, so your best defense is to punch first and punch hard. They won't expect you to be the aggressor," he advised.

Only one other time was I ever hassled, and fortunately it happened when I was with Monaco in a stairwell and late to class. As we cleared a landing and headed up the second flight, two large kids stood at the top, looking down at us with arms folded across their ample chests.

"Hey, fuckheads," they called. "You comin' up the down staircase. Turn your skinny asses around and do it right. Go around."

Looking up, Monaco quietly said, "I don't see any hall monitor badges." Monaco always talked just above a whisper.

"Yeah, keep comin' up these stairs and see who's in charge muthafucker," one said, smiling wickedly at his partner.

What happened next is still hard for me to believe, even though I was there and saw it with my one not-so-great eye. Zipping up the stairs, Monaco grabbed each by the throat and lifted them up and backward until they were pinned up against the hallway door. Their feet dangled helplessly an inch off the floor. Wordlessly, Monaco held them there until one croaked, "Okay, okay! We give!" After waiting another five seconds, Monaco released his hold, and both slid to the floor gasping for air.

"We better hustle or you'll be late to Typing," Monaco said. He wasn't even breathing hard.

Hanging with Monaco must have gotten to my head. Some months later, while on recess, I decided that, to prove my "badness,"

I was going to pick and win a fight with the biggest kid on the playground. Andre was a bit slow, but at six foot three he was physically well ahead of the curve for eighth graders. Because I was benchpressing my own weight and Monaco had given me a few boxing pointers, I was overconfident. It didn't go well. I shoved Andre and assumed my boxing stance, but when I threw the first punch it bounced harmlessly off his collarbone. I hadn't calculated that his height made punching him in the jaw nearly impossible. He simply wrapped me up in his huge arms and body-slammed me to the ground. And that quickly, the fight was over. When the teacher who supervised recess appeared, I was still trying to catch my breath and Big Andre had lumbered off to lunch.

When Monaco heard of my foolishness, he smiled his slight Dirty Harry smile and said, "Hermano, that was really stupid. But I bet no one fucks with you again." He was right. The remainder of my time at 217 was without any further bullying.

One unfortunate product of my time at Van Wyck, and my mother's own racist leanings, was I began to unconsciously develop an implicit bias against Black people. Nearly twenty years would pass before this bias revealed itself in dialogues I cofacilitated between Blacks and Latinos in higher education.

After I graduated PS 217, Dee and I moved, and I went to Richmond Hill High School (RHHS) in Queens. It also had a Sight Conservation class and, best of all, no busing; I could walk to school. It was there that I began to thrive. At the time, over half of the Latino kids in New York City's public schools dropped out. By contrast, I joined the student newspaper and the swim team, and founded the school's ecology club. In my senior year, I was even elected student government vice president. (I suspected that Mrs. Gold, the outspoken head of our Sight Conservation program, rigged the election.) Little did I suspect then that those four domains—writing, swimming, Mother Earth, and activism—would serve as touchstones for the next fifty years of my life.

The teachers at RHHS were highly motivated, and I began to flourish academically. Unlike so many other nondisabled Latino children in New York schools, the extra attention and resources I received for being disabled played a major part in my thriving. As my sight deteriorated, my math teacher, Mr. Sergey, tutored me in the very visual subject of geometry. He was also the advisor to the ecology club, and if you can imagine a six-foot-two skinny Cub Scout in tan shorts, that was Mr. Sergey. I initially struggled in geometry, unable to see the angles in the textbook. Yet with his hand-drawn, large-print worksheets and tests, I ended up scoring higher in my math SAT (the large-print version) than 90 percent of our class. He was a lovely man who was prouder of my eventual math scores than either I or my mother was.

Mr. Sergey was also the man who launched me on my first community organizing gig. As a school project, I'd gone by train to interview the management of the Indian Point nuclear power plant in Peekskill, New York, located only thirty-six miles upriver from New York City. I was curious about their thoughts on the upcoming first-ever Earth Day. My interview lasted about an hour, and I left convinced they were liars and nuclear power was not a safe energy alternative. That spring I organized, with Mr. Sergey's help, the school's first ecology club. On the first Earth Day, April 22, 1970, we conducted a cleanup of nearby Jamaica Bay Wildlife Refuge.

RHHS had been built in 1919. Though a showcase in earlier days, by 1970 the school had fallen into decay. The single-story wing of the school building that housed the pool had small glass windowpanes for a ceiling, and some kids thought tossing rocks at them to hear the glass shatter was fun. I recall watching the snowflakes hit my arms and dissolve as I swam endless laps during our afternoon swim practices. The temperature in the pool, built before the days of heated water, often fell below sixty degrees. Nevertheless, our coach had us doing mile after mile during practice, sometimes as many as twenty miles a week. It was not uncommon for one or two of us to run to the locker-room toilet, throw up, and come back and have to resume practice. Our most feared drill was the dreaded "100 Hundreds" workout: ten thousand yards, nearly six miles. But the intense rigor worked. We routinely competed on par with the legendary Bayside High swim team.

In 1971, our four-hundred-yard relay team was invited to participate in the prestigious New York City Semi-Finals swim meet. Our team consisted of a gifted freestyle swimmer named Mike, a very fast breaststroker named Carlos, a really tall and fast backstroker named Alex, and me, doing the hundred-yard butterfly to close out the relay.

Waiting to be called, I was beyond nervous. Our coach had disappeared, promising to be back before our heat. We suspected at the time that he'd gone to a bar around the corner. My anxiety only grew when an agitated official came up to us in the hallway and barked, "Where the hell is your coach? Your team's heat starts in two minutes! If you're not in position at the blocks you forfeit the heat."

Without our coach, our team captain, Mike, took charge and hustled us to the starting blocks, where we barely had time to strip off our sweats before the starter's gun sounded. Whether it was the adrenaline or being matched up against Bayside or something else, we opened a large lead. As it neared my turn to dive in and anchor the relay, we were well ahead of the five other teams in our heat, and swimming at a record pace.

Just then our absent coach appeared, smelling distinctly of beer, and yelled, "Bonilla, it's up to you!" I recall diving off the block with a five-yard lead and giving it my all for the first seventy-five yards. I was later told that my time, up to that point, exceeded my personal best by three full seconds. Then something happened. Whether it was the stress of being called at the last minute, the pressure inflicted by my drunken coach, or being in a city semifinal heat, I began struggling to breathe. Going into the last length with only ten yards left to race, I experienced a full-blown asthma attack. Panicking, I thought, "This can't be happening. I haven't had an asthma attack in years." I had reasoned, until then, that swimming had cured my asthma.

Unable to sustain my pace but determined not to stand up (which would have automatically disqualified us), and gasping and swallowing what seemed like a gallon of water, I somehow managed to limp to the finish line, placing a disappointing third. To the team's credit, they pulled me up out of the pool and, recognizing my condition, slapped me on the back and rubbed my wet, curly head.

Choking back tears, I apologized to my teammates and the coach. Mike leaned in close and whispered, "Not your fault, guy. And besides, we beat fuckin' Bayside!"

The following year the coach was replaced for drinking on the job, but we were unable to return to the City Semi-Finals in my senior year after Mike, our best freestyler, graduated. I later read growing up with a parent in an unfavorable mental health state, such as anxiety or stress, may predict a poorer status for a child's asthma. But swimming would forever set me apart from the label "disabled." It would continue to reinforce the importance of buoyancy in my life.

12. Bullies

CONVENTIONAL WISDOM suggests the cycle of bullying goes somewhat as follows:

The father gets chewed out at work by his boss.

The father comes home and then shoves the mother.

The mother then slaps the child for a minor infraction.

The child takes out his frustration by kicking the family dog.

My problem was, in elementary school I had no dog. But I did have Peter. He and I were in the notorious classroom 1C at Our Lady Queen of Martyrs, the class for slow kids. Peter's father ran the local pizzeria and Peter's friends often got free slices of their delicious, gooey Greek pizza. I guessed it was his dad's attempt to try and buy Peter some goodwill. Peter was tall for his age and overweight. He was shaped somewhat like a pear, narrow at the top and wide at the bottom. His large ears stuck out of the side of his head at an odd angle. They reminded us of a circus elephant, hence his unkind nickname, Dumbo. In today's lexicon, Peter would be labeled as mildly developmentally disabled.

Part of why I'd been placed with Peter in classroom IC was a nun who thought my Puerto Rican accent meant that I was somehow deficient. Even at eight, I knew I had no business being in a class for what my young self called "retarded" kids. To compound my frustration, although my mother and father were already separated, they continued to fight regularly about child support payments. Since my mother didn't yet have a dog, I was often the unlucky lone recipient of her dark rages.

And so it came to pass that Peter became an easy target for my misplaced anger. Peter had little athletic talent, so he was always picked last for anything having to do with team sports. To his credit, he never seemed bothered by this, nor did he respond to the frequent teasing we boys dished out with anything but a shy, silly grin.

On a drizzly Monday, following a difficult weekend where my father canceled a visitation I'd eagerly looked forward to, my better angels deserted me. Having recently suffered taunts myself for my being assigned to 1C, I snapped. As Peter and I and our two friends, brothers Jimmy and Johnny Lee, walked down a back alley on our way to school, I accidentally stepped into a fresh pile of dog excrement. As I cursed my nearsightedness, I heard Peter involuntarily giggling at my predicament. Although a big guy, Peter came across as a gentle giant, a trait we confused with being effeminate. When he was frightened (which was often), he'd let out a high-pitched scream that to our ears seemed "girly." Combined with my family and school frustrations and my homophobia, Peter became my dog.

Snatching some loose cardboard from a nearby dumpster, I swiftly scooped up some of the stinking dog poop and flung it at Peter. He was always slow to react, and it hit him square on the chest and rolled down his white uniform shirt, soiling his sky-blue OLQM school tie. He screamed in surprise and the other boys and I started chanting, "Shit stick, shit stick, Dumbo's got the shit stick!" Peter burst into tears. Watching as he lumbered awkwardly back down the alley toward his home, I immediately regretted what I'd done.

We didn't see Peter in school for the next two days. His family lived above the pizzeria, and on the third day after school, the Lee brothers and I visited the restaurant to see if I might make amends. Since it was early afternoon, it was still without customers. Peter's father was a short and stocky man who'd always treated us kindly, up until that day.

"Can Peter come out and play?" I asked meekly, standing by the cash register. Jimmy and Johnny were hanging back closer to the front doors.

As he leaned over the counter, Peter's father's bushy black eyebrows curled downward into a frown.

"No!" he barked. "Peter has been forbidden to play with you boys. I am very disappointed in all of you. I thought you were his friends. You are no longer welcome here unless accompanied by your parents." Pointing toward the restaurant's red double front doors, he commanded, "Leave. Now!"

I sensed Peter was in the kitchen just behind the swinging doors, listening, but he wouldn't show his face. Gulping down our embarrassment, the three of us slunk back out into the noise of Queens Boulevard, a busy eight-lane thoroughfare bisecting the borough. The rumbling and stink of the subway rising up from the steel grates of the sidewalk hit us as we slowly made our way down the street. A few weeks later we caught up with Peter as he made his way to school alone. He walked with us in silence, and gradually his shy smiled returned. As is the way with young children, we were soon back to playing together as if nothing had happened. We were never again treated to free pizza, but even then, that seemed an inadequate punishment for my misdeed.

The episode with Peter was a turning point in my young life. I never again made fun of Peter or of my other classmates with disabilities. In the years to come, I would make a career of standing up for people with disabilities and, later, any group that was treated unfairly based on their differences. But as they say about Karma, "What goes around comes around." I couldn't know then that within a year my Karma would come around, and I'd have to face violence directed my way for my difference.

* * *

In my early thirties, I'd attend a Latino men's group once a month in the conference room of Casa Latina in Northampton, Massachusetts. We explored manhood, sexism, and moments when we had to stand up for ourselves as Latinos. We'd sit in a circle around a dark walnut table and share our stories. The aroma of Café Bustelo filled the space. When my turn came, this was the bully story I shared.

It was the summer of 1965, about six months since my eye accident. It had been an exceptionally hot, humid, and sticky day. I was ten and attending the Catholic Youth Organization (CYO) day camp in Queens. They'd pick us up in a yellow school bus in the morning and drive us to local city parks for activities like ceramics, softball, and the very welcome free-swim period.

Near the end of my first week, I climbed into a crowded bus that smelled of sweaty kids and chlorine. There was only one seat left and it was way in the back. These were two-person bench seats, and to my dismay the window seat was occupied by the notorious Bully of CYO, Miguel. Miguel was older, half a head taller, and twenty pounds heavier than most of us other boys. His dark, curly hair fell over one eye, which gave him the appearance of a perpetually pissed-off, one-eyed pirate. Earlier in the week, I'd witnessed him shove a little kid to the ground so he could cut the line for midafternoon snacks. When the little boy stood up to protest, Miguel put his knee into the boy's groin.

"Ouch," groaned Raul, Casa's director. "That had to hurt." The room filled with the moans and the uneasy chuckles of men empathizing with the young boy's pain.

I continued: *The little guy didn't recover his breath for nearly five minutes, by which time all the afternoon snacks were gone. A female counselor came and tried to take Miguel to the office by grabbing his sweatshirt at the forearm. He ripped his arm out of her grip, shouting, "Yo, White bitch, don't be layin' your hands on me! You ain't my mother!" The first-year counselor stood haplessly by as Miguel straightened his sweatshirt and sauntered off.*

The circle of men all leaned forward, some with arms on the conference table, some with disbelieving looks on their faces. Outside, I could hear the soft pitter-patter of a spring rain hitting the windows.

So there I was on the bus with this juvenile delinquent, and he was spread out over three-quarters of the only seat left on the entire bus. So as to not provoke him, I carefully tried to slide my butt sideways onto the remaining quarter of the bench. He then turned and whipped his feet onto the entire bench, making it impossible for me to sit.

"Coño," cursed Raul. "What did you do?" Outside, a rumble of thunder punctuated his question.

I went on, *The bus was beginning to move and I needed to sit down so as not to get in trouble with the driver. I pressed my hips onto the edge of the bench attempting to slide in again, but Miguel used both his feet to firmly shove me off the bench. I landed unceremoniously in the center aisle to a chorus of laughter from the other kids. I wasn't hurt, but I was embarrassed, scared, and now pissed off. I pleaded with him, "Come on, dude, this is the last seat, and we're not allowed to stand."*

He abruptly stopped laughing and hissed, "Mira, puta, this is my seat. Sit here again and I'll mess you up bad. I don't care if you're blind, or whatever."

Incredulous, Francisco, another group member, asked, "Really? He threatened a blind kid?"

Miguel's rep left no doubt in my mind. I looked around desperately for a counselor. No such luck. I was out of options. In an attempt to mask how intimidated I felt, and perhaps to call over a counselor, I shouted, "There's no other seats, so I'm sitting! Please move your feet." Assured of the outcome, Miguel began to stand, preparing to give me a beatdown. But he never got the chance.

"Didn't a counselor intervene? Didn't the bus driver stop the bus?" asked Raul. Outside, the rain came down harder, but inside Casa Latina the only sound was the coffee pot percolating.

In that moment my boxing advice from Monaco Baez came to me. My first punch was a roundhouse right that caught Miguel squarely on his left cheek. The force of it, combined with his shock at being hit by a "gimp," knocked him backward onto the bench. Then I let loose as if my life depended on it. I rained punches on that boy . . . left-right, left-right, left-right, all delivered faster than I imagined possible. It had to be the adrenaline kicking in. The other kids on the bus were screaming, "Fight, fight!" Even though he covered his face with his arms, I still managed to box both his ears in good.

"Where'd you learn to fight?" asked Francisco.

"By watching my friend Monaco's brother train for Golden Gloves at Madison Square Garden."

The kids on the bus hadn't expected this turn of events. Finally a reluctant counselor made his way to the back of the bus, but it was all over. The Bully of CYO was huddled on the floor like a limp sack of flour. The only sound on the bus was his sobbing and an occasional hiccup.

Seeing the danger had passed, I began to shake and my legs felt like Jell-O.

"Did you get into trouble with the counselors?" asked Francisco. "Were you kicked out of CYO?"

After they attended to Miguel, the head counselor commanded me to go to the front and take his seat. "We'll deal with you later," he said. He sat next to Miguel for the remainder of the trip. As I made my way up to the front of the bus the looks on the faces of the campers startled me. Rather than applause or cheers, which is what you might expect for taking down the camp bully, their faces were a mixture of wonder, but also dread. Instead of being elated at having avoided a beating, a cold chill came over me. They're afraid of me! They think I'm the new Bully of CYO. Oddly, I never got into any trouble for the fight. From that day on no one dared pick on me, but no one befriended me either."

Shaking his head from side to side, Raul leaned away from the table and back into his chair. "That seems unfair. You defend yourself and you're the one ostracized?" The other men around nodded. "What eventually happened?" Raul asked.

"My last two days at camp were uneventful, but lonesome. That night over a dinner of my Nana's arroz con pollo and tostones I told her my story."

Nana said, "Jovencito, it's going to be lonely being different and yet strong in this world. You need to get used to it. Be strong anyhow." Her words would be the foundation on which I learned not only perseverance but also resilience.

Many of us had nanas who had touched our Spirits with their gentle wisdom. Nana's advice elicited head nods from my gathered Latino 'manos.

13. Puerto Rico's Hatfields versus the McCoys

THE RED, WHITE, AND BLUE BUNTING decorating the grandstand flutters gently in the soft Caribbean breeze. Emerging from the assembled crowd, the assassin races toward the outdoor reviewing stand, a .45-caliber handgun at his side. Governor Blanton Winship, the unelected Anglo bureaucrat overseeing the colonial occupation of Puerto Rico, sees the oncoming specter of death and freezes. Twenty feet from the grandstand the Puerto Rican Independista raises his deadly weapon and takes aim.

Just as he pulls the trigger, a young colonel, Luis Irizarry of the Puerto Rican National Guard, already seated on the grandstand, leaps in front of the governor. The colonel's heroic action saves the governor's life but costs Irizarry his own.

* * *

One witness to these events was Colonel Irizarry's nine-year-old son, Luis Jr., who remained seated on the grandstand next to his dying father's body. It was July 25, 1938. President Franklin Delano Roosevelt would remove Governor Winship from office the following year for malfeasance. Today, the National Guard armory in Yauco bears Colonel Irizzary's name. He was my mother's cousin, my grandfather's nephew.

As a result of this assassination, my mother's side of the family became passionately anti-independence and supported the U.S. occupation. My father's family, on the other hand, were widely known sympathizers of the Independista movement. So much so that my grandfather, Don Bernadino, made Pedro Albizu Campos, the fiery leader of the Independista movement, my father's godfather.

In 1950, twelve years after the attempted assassination of Governor Winship, Albizu Campos was believed to have sent two squads of Independistas to Washington, D.C. One squad shot up the halls of Congress, wounding several representatives. Simultaneously, the second squad killed a security guard at Blair House while President Truman slept upstairs unharmed.

For some on the island, these were seen as acts of protest against the U.S. colonial occupation. Others, like my mother's family, saw the actions of the Independistas as acts of terrorism. My grandfather's support of the independence movement had already cost him business for his struggling photography studio, and after the attacks on Congress and Blair House, matters went from bad to worse. Escalating death threats would eventually force the family to flee north to Nueva York. Once in the United States, as if in reaction to his father's political leanings, my father became a bedrock Republican. In turn, I would later become sympathetic to all oppressed peoples, including Puerto Ricans.

For decades the details of our family's Puerto Rican version of the Hatfields versus the McCoys remained a closely guarded secret until after the deaths of both Don Bernadino and Doña Luisa. In the midst of my research into our family's history, my mother finally told me the saga of the secret feud.

She said that one night while visiting Puerto Rico she ran into her cousin, Luis Irizarry Jr., at the Fort Buchanan military base officers club. "After watching his father shot down in front of his eyes little Luis Jr. grew up to be a very unstable man. Between you and me," she said, "he's a basket case."

To my disappointment, my mother became highly critical of my activism and later community organizing. I took her judgmental attitude personally and saw it as a manifestation of her internalized colonialism and racism. It wasn't until researching my family's history that I began to understand the origins of her objection.

I'd never known that my father's godfather was a revolutionary fighting colonial oppression. At twenty, after learning the story, I began to understand the source of my own fire for social justice, and I felt validated and emboldened. My mother trembled at the idea of the violence embodied in our two families' secret feud, and she worried on my behalf. My resentment of her lack of support began to soften. But my own initiation into political action would begin, unlikely enough, due to a teenage infatuation.

*　*　*

Shouts of "Fight the power! Fight the power!" filled the over-crowded lobby of the Lighthouse for the Blind's Manhattan head-quarters. Fifty blind teenagers were engaged in a sit-in at the glass office tower owned by the New York Association for the Blind on Fifty-ninth Street.

Drawn by the chanting and drumming inside, a crowd of curi-ous passersby gathered on the sidewalk outside. Two enormous security guards stood at the front doors, arms crossed over their muscular chests, unsure of what to do. Although pumped, I kept a wary eye on the nervous guards. It was the winter of 1970, I was fif-teen, and this was my first protest rally. I'd been talked into partici-pating by our protest's leader, Maureen O'Brien.

Maureen was three years my senior. During my first day at the Lighthouse's Saturday rec program, she'd taken me on a "forbid-den" lunch by urging me to leave the building and join her across the street at the local Greek deli. Not wanting to seem chicken and badly wanting to impress her, I'd said "Sure." Consequences be damned. Maureen was not only older, she was drop-dead gorgeous, red-haired, and every bit the Irish beauty her name connoted. Little wonder I had a crush.

As we headed for the exit, our brown bags of falafel sandwiches and sodas in hand, I promptly walked headfirst into the deli's closed glass door. I lay sprawled on the tile floor, more embarrassed than seriously hurt. Though totally blind, Maureen immediately knew what happened and snarked, "I bet you don't make that mistake again." Three weeks later, Maureen talked me into yet another ad-venture.

"Bonilla, don't you want a say in the music that gets spun for our supposed dance hour?" she demanded to know. She knew that I loved to dance and that the lack of Motown and salsa played by the staff was a sore point for me and several of the other participants. She added, "Most of the participants are Black and Brown while the staff here are all White like me, and all sighted."

As the rally got up a head of steam, a rattled front-desk receptionist vainly tried to quiet our energized group. "We demand a face-to-face with Cione," Maureen yelled over the receptionist's pleas for calm. This was immediately followed by chants of "We want Cione! We want Cione!" Nick Cione was the new Saturday recreation program director. Several rounds of "We Shall Overcome" later, a smiling Cione stepped off an elevator to address the protesters.

He agreed to meet with the group only on the condition that we move the sit-in out of the front lobby and into a small first-floor auditorium (presumably out of sight of the gawkers on Fifty-ninth Street). Nick was twenty-seven years old and smelled of patchouli cologne. With his braid and short leather vest, he reminded me of Jerry Garcia.

Maureen began the meeting. "We've staged the walkout from this afternoon's activities to protest the lack of blind staff as well as participant input into programming," she said. With me as a backup, Maureen negotiated for our right to control the turntable, and Nick promised Lighthouse would hire more blind staffers within a year.

As we dispersed in victory, wide-eyed, I turned to Maureen and whispered, "What a rush!" Unknown to anyone at the time, I would eventually become the first blind counselor ever hired by Lighthouse for their summer camp on the Jersey Shore.

*   *   *

My second foray into the world of disability activism came five years later in California, two years after my sight was surgically corrected. By then a staffer for a recreation program for disabled children and adults in San Francisco, I came to understand firsthand how crucial transportation services were to people with disabilities. In a shocking act of fiscal conservatism, then-Governor Jerry Brown, citing budget constraints, chose to cut state funds for transportation for people with disabilities, which meant no access to our programs.

In response, the center I worked for co-organized a caravan to Sacramento to stage a surprise takeover of Brown's office. The sight of sixty blind and disabled people, many of them in wheelchairs, barricading themselves in the governor's reception area made for great photo ops. When a press conference was called on the capitol steps, the governor's state police contingent saw their chance to clear the reception area. What they didn't count on was the sheer weight and volume of our older-model electric wheelchairs, especially when occupied.

I'd had to leave the capitol steps and return to the reception area to retrieve meds for one of my participants. Another staff member named Donna joined me. Seeing what the troopers were about to do, I positioned myself in a chair, pretending to be its owner. A particularly large member of the governor's protective detail approached me. Wearing the obligatory trooper campaign hat, he was clearly the Man in Charge. Standing close to six feet six, he must've tipped the scales at over 250 pounds, all of it muscle.

In front of Donna, he leaned over me and brusquely said, "Get up."

I meekly replied, "Can't."

"Get up or I'll throw you out of that chair. Get up, now!" he repeated.

While his steely gray eyes blazed with anger, my kidneys began to scream for relief. Standing nearby, Donna pleaded, "He really can't, leave him alone."

The trooper first looked at her and then back at me—hard. We'd interrupted their planned clearing of the offices, and now he was unsure of their next move. In a hoarse whisper I turned to Donna and said, "You better get Jan." Jan was the program director coordinating our part of the sit-in.

Off Donna dashed and for several long minutes I waited for reinforcements, during which time the giant trooper and I exchanged glances. A contingent of eight large troopers had gathered in the hallway. Suddenly the distinctive whirring of electric wheelchairs echoed down the marble hallway. The cavalry was arriving! They easily skirted the troopers, who were clearly uncomfortable with blocking people in wheelchairs, and our group once again filled the reception area. A song arose from the group, "We Shall Not Be Moved," just in time for the arrival of the print and television media, including their photographers and camera people.

While I waited for reinforcements, I'd been so scared that even if I'd wanted to vacate the chair my legs wouldn't have complied. The sense of relief at the arrival of my fellow activists broke over me like a wave. Sensing they'd lost the element of surprise and unwilling to bodily carry disabled people in wheelchairs out of the reception area in front of the press, the governor's security detail retreated to wild applause.

I was roundly congratulated as people clapped me on the back. Excusing myself, I went in search of the closest bathroom stall, where I promptly threw up my lunch. Sadly, that particular day we lost the battle, as Governor Brown followed through on his threatened cuts. My takeaway? When you oppose the powers that be it will be scary, do it anyway—but to be on the safe side, eat a light lunch.

14.   Camp Lighthouse

B EING LEGALLY BLIND, I learned early to embrace the value of all my senses. Mother Earth became my Teacher and my Consoler, and the outdoors my classroom and church. Prior to my sit-in adventure at the New York Association for the Blind, I attended their Saturday recreation program in Manhattan. It was there that I first heard about Camp Lighthouse. It was 1970, and that summer I became a camper at the camp's site on the New Jersey shore.

On my third night, it was swelteringly muggy and I couldn't sleep. Unbeknown to my snoring counselor and cabinmates, in a sudden blaze of bravado I slipped silently outside. I could see well enough to notice that the moon was full, and it lit my path almost as well as a Queens streetlight. I decided to go on a solo walkabout until I got sleepy again. Barefoot, following the braille fence posts, I could feel the gravel of the path crunch softly underfoot. From what I could tell, I was the only person stirring in the camp.

Hearing the buzzing drone of mosquitos, I opted to head to the beach, where I hoped the sea breeze might discourage the hungry pests. A competitive swimmer, I decided on a whim to go for a skinny dip and then sneak back into Cabin C before anyone was any the wiser. Swimming alone was strictly verboten at the camp, but so was leaving one's cabin in the middle of the night. And at fifteen, I was craving some alone time and reveled in the freedom of escaping the noise, rules, and commotion that was my first summer camp experience.

In the moonlight I followed the guide rails that led out to Barnegat Bay via a half-mile-long boardwalk. I kept my right hand atop the splintery guardrail as I moved, but halfway to the beach I was suddenly stopped in my tracks. The clomp, clomp, clomp of my footfalls on the cedar boards had been gradually overwhelmed by a cacophony of sounds unfamiliar to a Nuyorican boy's ears.

A chorus of croaking bullfrogs filled the moist night air, immediately followed by the distinctive call of the elusive whippoorwill. Not far in the distance, I could hear the shrieking of herring gulls near the bay. The ether was pungent with the smell of rotten eggs common to swamp gas. Pausing, I realized that I was standing just inches above a salt marsh typical of the Pine Barrens region of New Jersey's southern shore.

The camp was situated within the largest remaining example of the Atlantic Coast's pine barrens ecosystem. Despite its proximity to Philadelphia, and being only ninety miles from my New York City home, the Pine Barrens remain mostly rural and undisturbed. It earned the name because of the sandy, acidic soil that prevented European settlers from cultivating their familiar crops. But the unique ecology of the Pine Barrens harbors a remarkable diversity of plant life, including orchids and carnivorous vegetation like pitcher plants, sundews, and bladderworts. That night I sensed tiny creatures stirring just under my feet in the brackish waters.

Tasting salt on my lips, I realized that out here, in the middle of the night, in the middle of a marsh, amid the wilds of the Pine Barrens, Nature was embracing me. I felt goosebumps run up and down my forearms, and the hairs on the nape of my neck stiffened. I was being reminded that I was never alone. The irony that I'd originally come seeking solitude was not lost on me.

After a long couple of minutes drinking in the place, I proceeded down the boardwalk to the beach. After cooling off with a swim, I sat on the dock and let the warm sea wind dry me. I watched as the moon reflected off the waves as the tide rolled in, Otis Redding's "(Sittin' on) The Dock of the Bay" playing in my head. After putting my clothes back on, like a ninja, I silently slipped back into my bunk, refreshed and reassured by my marsh adventure into the

sweet darkness. Five decades later a friend would send me a poem
by David Whyte that brought that night back to me:

Sweet Darkness

When your eyes are tired
the world is tired also.

When your vision has gone,
no part of the world can find you.

Time to go into the dark
where the night has eyes
to recognize its own.

There you can be sure
you are not beyond love.

The dark will be your home
tonight.

The night will give you a horizon
further than you can see.

You must learn one thing.
The world was made to be free in.

Give up all the other worlds
except the one to which you belong.

Sometimes it takes darkness and the sweet
confinement of your aloneness
to learn

anything or anyone
that does not bring you alive

is too small for you.

*   *   *

The camp director placed his long bony fingers on my shoulder and squeezed. Roger Rush stood about six feet three inches tall and looked and sounded like a Southern version of Ichabod Crane. It was just after breakfast and I was sitting in the director's small office just off the dining room. I could smell the aroma of bacon wafting through the shiplap walls.

"Jimmy, you could be the first blind camper ever to become a counselor," Roger said.

His offer struck me as remarkable given this was a camp for the blind. I was an exceptionally high-functioning camper, being partially sighted in my right eye. But in the fifty years of the camp's existence, I would be the first camper hired as staff. My ego swelled at the thought of Roger's seeming regard for me. I was motivated to take the offered counselor-in-training position for many reasons: to prove myself; to escape New York City's sweltering, crime-ridden summers; to make some money for college; and to flee my mother's clutches. The last was the issue that my mother latched onto that night in a highly charged phone call home to let her know of my good news.

"It's amazing to me. How you're just like your father," she said. "Just thinking of yourself. How can you even think of abandoning your mother alone in New York? Of course you can't stay all summer. I expect you home Friday night." Friday was my last scheduled day as a camper.

In an unusual flash of boldness, I sputtered, "I don't understand. Why aren't you happy for me? It's a once-in-a-lifetime opportunity. I'm taking this job and you can't stop me."

"What, you expect to leave me in this apartment for the rest of the summer all alone? Jimmy, you're incredible. You have no loyalty, no sense of responsibility. At times like this I wonder if you weren't accidentally switched at birth at the hospital."

I explained how it would be a great experience for the purposes of my proposed college major, therapeutic recreation. I emphasized how much I would learn and earn.

"Fine! Go live at that God-damned camp," she shouted. "And when it's over, go live with your father and his mother. See if he'll want to take you in, a child with a disability!" As she talked her breathing came faster and faster.

My mind raced. How might I wrangle my last two years of high school while living with my father and grandmother in Fort Lee, New Jersey? My high school was in Queens, and I soon realized the improbability of this scenario. I felt my own breath getting short as panic began to creep up from my belly.

On the other end of the line my mother continued to berate me, drawing comparisons to my "useless" father and then her own father. "You're just like them! Selfish, selfish, selfish! Go live with your father. See how willing he'll be to assume responsibility for a blind child." For the umpteenth time, she regaled me with her "horror stories" of taking him to court.

"God knows your pathetic excuse for a father wouldn't even pay child support unless the judge threatened to put him in jail."

I gave it one last desperate try. "Dee, it's only seven weeks. It's only seven weeks."

"Either you come home this Friday or I send your things to your grandmother. I'm done talking with you, you, you . . . ungrateful thing. ¡Tú eres sinvergüenza!" (You are without shame!)

On that note, she slammed the phone down in my ear. Standing just outside the camp office, I trembled as I slowly hung up the pay phone receiver. Aware that there were people milling about nearby, I held back my tears. It was hard catching my breath, and my hands and legs suddenly felt numb. I needed to be alone.

It was well after dinner and getting dark as I stumbled out to the boardwalk that led to the bay. After a quarter mile I reached the wooden pavilion at the halfway point. It looked out onto the marsh. As I lowered myself onto the weathered gray wooden bench, the sound of bullfrogs, the smell of swamp gas, and the taste of salty air permeated my senses. The frogs abruptly stopped croaking as an unexpected wail escaped my throat. The terror of total abandonment and possible homelessness crashed over me like the angry waves at Long Beach Island. I sat weeping. Eventually, I was shaken from my despair by an enormous orange moon rising over the darkened wetlands. My terror and loneliness were temporarily replaced by a sense of awe.

Cried out, I resumed my walk and finally reached the end of the boardwalk at Barnegat Bay. I was so exhausted I curled up onto a long narrow shelf that surrounded the dock. With the stars and the warm sea breeze as my only comforters, I fell into a restless sleep. My ears filled with the echo of the waves lapping the dock's pylons below.

I awoke to the cry of herring gulls circling overhead. The dawn had turned the dunes and sandy shore a warm amber color. Stiff, damp, and cold, I climbed down from my night's perch. The morning's beauty and tranquil water calmed me. Remembering my predicament, I somehow found myself less desperate, less alone, and more resolved to stay at Camp Lighthouse.

After breakfast I went to Roger's office and the previous evening's drama spilled out of me. As a male figure of authority, I hoped he might be listened to by Dee. In his distinctive South Carolinian accent, he said, "I'll smooth things out with Dinorah. I'll give her the rest of the day to calm down and then call her tonight."

The relief I felt mixed with an immense sense of gratitude as I returned to my cabin to catch a quick cat nap before morning activities. At dinner Roger came to my cabin's table and leaned in close to my ear. He whispered, "Come to my cabin after evening program. I'll have news for you." With that teaser he moved off to sit at the senior camp staff table. Several times I noticed him looking over at me and smiling.

That night I could barely control my desire for evening program to end. Roger's cabin was about two hundred yards from the camp compound and afforded the director some privacy. When I knocked on his door I heard a cheery "Y'all come in." Entering, I saw Roger wasn't alone. A senior counselor named Joe was sitting at Roger's table drinking beer. Joe was older than the other counselors—I guessed him to be between twenty-five and thirty. Roger was sprawled on his bed wearing only short-shorts with a large gold chain hanging around his neck that made the wispy build of his chest seem all the scrawnier. Both men had skipped evening program, and it was clear they had been drinking. Roger in particular seemed very drunk, making his Southern drawl even more pronounced than usual.

"Jimmy my boy," he slurred. "I have good news for you."

Quietly, Joe came up from behind and locked the cabin door. Sitting up on the edge of his cot, Roger's watery eyes took on a creepy, leering look. I simultaneously experienced two conflicting sensations, a huge sense of elation but also a mounting sense of alarm.

"Your mama and I talked," Roger said. "I convinced her that this job was a great professional opportunity. I told her she should be proud that she raised you and that you'll be the first blind counselor in camp history. I also promised I'd keep a close eye on y'all."

I could hear the sound of my heart thumping in my chest. I instinctively scanned the room for exits.

"Why don't you all come over here and let me get a good look at you."

My dress code for camp was like that of all the other male campers and counselors, a T-shirt, sandals, and a bathing suit.

"Thanks, Roger, but I'd better get back to my cabin," I said. "Ralph"—my senior counselor—"will be wondering where I am."

Suddenly Joe was behind me, all six foot two of him, and he pinned my arms to my sides. Although I religiously lifted weights, I wasn't strong enough to break his grip. He then inched me forward toward Roger, whose long, skinny fingers started to fumble at the strings of my bathing suit. My stomach was turning in knots.

"My, my, I bet your cock is the envy of all the gals at camp. Let me take a good look," he wheezed in a hoarse whisper. With no forethought, I used Joe behind me as a brace and, rising up, kicked out and planted my right foot squarely on the bridge of Roger's nose. The sound of cracking cartilage and Roger's yips of pain filled the small cabin. Joe, startled by the sudden turn of events, loosened his grip just long enough for me to twist out of his grasp. Like my own cabin, the large screen window in this room had a latch that opened out.

Roger ordered Joe, "Find me a towel. Find me a towel! I'm bleeding like a stuck pig!"

Caught between grabbing me and responding to Roger's distress call, Joe hesitated. That was long enough for me to flip the screen latch and catapult myself out the window. Landing on the soft duff of the hemlock trees, I was shaking, but also laughing at the stunned expression on Roger's pale face. I suppose it was my way of coping—what I came to call "hysterical bravado." On feathery legs, I ran back to my cabin assured that no one would molest me in a cabin full of blind campers blessed with acute hearing. Still, I struggled to get my heart rate in check. It was the familiar call of the whippoorwill that calmed me down long enough to drift off into a restless, guarded sleep.

The next morning as I entered the mess hall for breakfast, I spied Joe and Roger. They were sitting at a table at the far end of the dining room, alone and obviously nursing their hangovers. There was a large gauze bandage over Roger's nose. One eye was blue-black and turning an ugly shade of yellow. Later I confirmed from Dee that he'd convinced her to let me work at the camp for the summer. For the rest of camp neither Roger nor Joe paid me any mind. It would be my last run-in with them, but not the last time Roger and I would work together. Years later, at a camp called Jened, I'd warn the younger male counselors to never go to his cabin at night under any circumstances.

A reasonable person might question why I would even consider working with Roger again. But from my life with Dee, I absorbed an important lesson: that social connections are critical to accessing opportunities. Well before my fateful encounter in Roger's cabin, he had proven to be a significant mentor. One of his stories left a major impression on me. It was about the time he had been working as a recreation therapist at New York's Rehabilitation Institute in Manhattan. He had been a member of a rehab team that included doctors, psychiatrists, and physical and occupational therapists.

One of the team's clients was a former police officer who had been rendered paralyzed by a robber's bullet. After eighteen months of intensive therapy, the team voted on whether this client was rehabilitated enough to be released on his own. The officer had learned to use his prosthetic arms well enough to perform a range of activities of daily living, including feeding himself and driving. Roger, a recreation therapist, was the lone dissenting voice to argue that the officer wasn't prepared to be sent out on his own. But Roger was overruled and, along with tens of thousands of dollars of expensive adaptive equipment, the officer was released, complete with a state-of-the-art prosthetic hand. Sadly, within a month, the news reached the team that the man had used his newly outfitted prosthetic hand to put his service revolver to his head and kill himself.

Roger's story of the police officer was a turning point for me regarding the value of therapeutic recreation as a career. It started me investigating internships, and later colleges, that offered rec therapy as a major. Two years after our encounter in the cabin, Roger would write me a glowing letter of recommendation that helped assure my acceptance to SUNY Cortland's therapeutic recreation program. Even though his alcoholism forced me to forfeit my trust in him, I intuited he would still be a vital link for me to a wider world.

Recently, I listened to a program on National Public Radio's *Hidden Brain* on the value of social connectivity. One piece of the program helped explain my relationship with Roger. The research showed that poor people and people of color often do not have access to social connections that open doors available to middle- and upper-class Americans. Reflecting back, it hit me that no one in my immediate family had ever gone to college or encouraged me to do so. It was partly Roger's mentorship that solidified my career choice and led me to opt for college.

It was true that Roger had tried to sexually assault me. But he was, ironically, also a vehicle that opened unimagined opportunities for this young working-class Puerto Rican. Like Dee, who had facilitated many good things on my behalf, Roger also proved to be an unpredictably dangerous force in my life. Rather than only seeing the Bad or Good in life, I was coming to appreciate something Henry David Thoreau once wrote: "Truth is always paradoxical."

15. The Gift of Not Seeing

B LINDNESS DIDN'T JUST HAPPEN *TO* ME; it also happened *for* me. Camp Lighthouse featured a nature program that culminated with an overnight campout. Unlike at Lighthouse's Manhattan headquarters, volunteers at Camp Lighthouse were a rarity. One memorable volunteer was Henry. A bear of a man, Henry would bring his animals to camp for the blind campers to touch. Rabbits, goats, horses, sheep, baby chickens, you name it, Henry had it. He was a gentle soul who had a gift for inspiring trust not just with his many animals, but with us city kids as well. I was in my second season at Camp Lighthouse as a counselor in training when Henry offered his three-acre farm site as a campout location, and I quickly enlisted. There, in a small meadow opposite his animal pens, we erected several six-person tents.

This year there was a new female counselor who had joined the staff. Her name was May. It was all the male counselors could do not to have their tongues lolling out of their mouths at the sight of her. To me, being partially sighted, she looked like Cheryl Tiegs in a soft, oversized red flannel shirt and denim shorts. What lingers with me still is the softness of her voice. May was nineteen. Now a senior counselor, I was eighteen.

After dinner and the requisite campfire sing-along we retired to our respective tents. Because tent space was limited and there were few female campers on this trip, May ended up in my tent with three campers. The night was hot and humid and we all slept on top of our sleeping bags. Once the flashlights had been turned off I settled into a fidgety sleep.

I don't remember how it first happened. Her bag was next to mine. I recall falling asleep, and somewhere in the middle of the night I must have turned over with my arm outstretched. Accidentally, in the dark, I touched May's hand. At the first contact with her fingers, an intense sensation like a crack of electricity shot down my arm. Embarrassed, I froze. I couldn't see, but I knew she must be lying on her side facing me. Then, to my astonishment, her hand opened and her fingers gently intertwined with mine. After a few breathless moments, I began to softly caress the length of her palm. As my fingertips explored hers, I discovered a small protuberance on her right thumb.

Whispering so as to not disturb our tentmates, I asked "Does it hurt?" I heard her laugh quietly and say, "No, it's just a wart. It doesn't hurt."

Before we'd retired for the night and because of the heat, May had taken off her flannel top. Gathering my courage, slowly I ran my fingers up the length of her bare forearm. She lay stock-still, saying nothing, not withdrawing from my touch. Her naked shoulders excited me, but I chose instead to touch her face, her peach-like cheeks, soft eyebrows, nose, and full lips. Unexpectedly, a camper next to me moaned in their sleep, causing me to pull back my hand.

In a hushed, hoarse tone May said, "It's okay, you don't have to stop."

The humid air was heavy with the smell of Henry's goats. I thought, *I've died and gone to heaven.* Carefully, gradually, I returned my hand to caress her chin and neck. I brushed her blond hair back as I continued to stroke her neck and then her clavicle. The silence was profound—the only sound was the occasional snore of a camper in the tent next to ours. May was wearing a dance leotard beneath her shirt, so I traced its neckline with my pinky. I heard her breath catch and I hesitated. In response, her hand touched my face and lips, and I kissed her fingertips. The palm of my hand unintentionally grazed her erect nipple and I could feel my own hardness swell. I'd had yet to make love to a woman and I dared imagine this might be the night, tentmates all but forgotten.

Suddenly there was a stirring outside our tent. A voice said, "Brother Bonilla, are you there? It's Rick. I have to go pee." Rick, who was totally blind, was one of my friends and was in a different tent. Duty-bound (like a chump), I rose quickly, unzipped our tent flap, and escorted him to the latrine on the opposite side of the meadow. When I returned ten minutes later, my flashlight revealed May had turned over. I dared not reapproach her.

Had it all been a dream? Dream or not, my moment with the camp beauty was over. And Rick was none the wiser—damn his weak bladder!

16. Mr. Norton, MSW

A T SIXTEEN I'd been legally blind for seven years, but this was the first time I'd stepped into the cavernous offices of New York State's Department of Vocational Rehabilitation Services. I was in a section of Queens dominated by old brick warehouses and abandoned factories, not a neighborhood you'd want to be caught wandering alone in at night. As a precaution, I'd stashed the monocular I used to see approaching trains in my coat pocket. Thanks to a recent six-week garbage strike, trash overflowed from cans lining the curbs along the way. Finding the building, I took the creaky, musty elevator up to the third floor.

The receptionist at the lobby desk asked, "Name?" A blue cloud of cigarette smoke curled above her bleach-blond hair. Her perfume called to mind overly ripe bananas. I told her my name.

"And what's your business here?" Despite wearing an outfit designed for a twentysomething, the timbre of her voice betrayed the fact that she was well into her forties.

I explained I was there to see my vocational rehab counselor, Mr. Norton. "The appointment was made by Mr. Nick Cione of the Lighthouse," I added to sound a bit more official.

"Elevators are to the left. Fourth floor and take a left. He's at the end of the hall on the right." She went back to her typing, never once having looked up.

I exited on the fourth floor. The walls were a study of pasty gray and muddy green. The wooden floors were old and scuffed and probably dated back to the building's days as a hat factory. Mr. Norton's office door had frosted glass on the upper half. A fading plaque with large lettering on the door read, MR. J. NORTON MSW. It included braille lettering below his name. I knocked.

A hoarse voice said, "Come in. You must be my four o'clock. Come in, come in." Mr. Norton, clearly unsure of my visual ability, directed me around the small office. "There's a chair to your right at ten o'clock." Getting seated across from his desk, I got a closer look at my new Vocational Rehabilitation counselor. He had a short Afro peppered with lots of gray and a heavy four o'clock shadow, also showing gray. The air in the office smelled of cigarettes and burnt coffee. The place oozed a weary vibe.

"James, is it? How can I help?" It was a question he'd probably posed hundreds of times before, and he delivered it with little enthusiasm.

"Mrs. Gold, my Sight Conservation teacher at PS 133, told me that to qualify for college financial aid I have to formally meet with a representative of the state office of Voc Rehab and get their okay."

Mr. Norton was that representative. Without standing, he swiveled his chair from around his desk to come closer to where I was sitting. "James, you realize that college isn't right for most of my clients. What do you want to go to college for?" His tone was flat, betraying neither judgment nor hostility. Without pausing to hear my response, he turned back to his desk and grabbed a file from atop a large stack of manila folders. In the process, he nearly knocked a full ashtray off the desk. He opened the file and leafed through the pages.

"This is your lucky day, James," he said. It was the first hint of a smile I'd seen since our interview began. "This just came in just today. I can place you in your own kiosk by Grand Central Station starting next September. It's a prime moneymaking location and it'll provide you a very tidy livelihood. Believe you me young man, this is a once-in-a-lifetime opportunity. If I were you I'd snap it up before somebody else does." The soft smile on his face conveyed a combination of benevolence and satisfaction.

"Gee, thanks, sir. But I plan to attend SUNY Cortland in the fall. What I really need is your signature that certifies I'm legally blind and eligible for state and federal financial aid." I pulled out the appropriate form from my daypack.

Mr. Norton's eyebrows arched downward. I sensed surprises didn't happen often in his line of work. He paused to light a cigarette. I couldn't see the pack's lettering, but Camels were my father's brand, so I instantly recognized the distinctive aroma and red-and-white packaging.

Holding up the file, he said, "Well, I'd give this serious consideration if I were you. There's no guarantee that even with a college degree you'll ever come close to earning this kind of income." With that he pushed his swivel chair back behind his desk and stared into the file.

"Thanks, but I plan to be a recreational therapist and work with people with disabilities. Kind of like what you do. If you could just sign here, I'll be on my way." I proffered him the page to sign. Nick at Lighthouse had coached me to get a signature on the spot or else I might wait months for the bureaucracy to process the simple paperwork.

Although Mr. N was sitting farther from my field of sight, I could see his head slowly shaking. It was closing in on five o'clock and I was probably his last appointment of the day. Sensing he was ready to go home while it was still light out, I asked, "Can you possibly sign it today so I can take it with me?"

He paused a second, then reached across his desk and took the paperwork. He crushed out the cigarette he had just lit, picked up a blue Bic ballpoint from his green felt blotter, and scrawled his name and the date.

"Let me walk you out toward the copy machine so I can get a copy for my records," he said. He stood slowly, with effort, and came out from behind the desk. We took a short walk to a copier I had passed earlier on my way in. With a practiced motion, he made his copy and handed me back the original.

"Good luck, young man. Let me know how that college thing works out. If not, I'm sure I'll have something available. Perhaps not at Grand Central, but something." He pressed the elevator down button for me.

The elevator door opened, and while riding back down to the first floor, I felt a sadness wash over me. I had a sense that I'd never see Mr. Norton nor the Voc Rehab building again. I bet Mr. Norton once loved his job. Now it seemed he was going through the motions just waiting for his state retirement pension. Though I was relieved he'd signed my form, the man had come very close to tracking me into a dead-end job. I vowed to myself that I'd never be the kind of professional that would become a victim of institutional ableism. We couldn't foresee that within my lifetime, newspaper kiosks would largely become obsolete in the digital age. Small wonder blind people remain among the poorest of the poor, especially Black and Brown blind folk.

Zipping my jacket against the cold, I stepped out into the wind that was blowing down the garbage-strewn street. I hurried to the El subway stop staircase before the darkening gray clouds unleashed a cold rain, a rain that would help wash the stench from the streets.

17. Florida School for the Deaf and Blind

V ACATIONING IN ST. AUGUSTINE in 2018, on a whim I spontaneously attended an open house at the Florida School for the Deaf and Blind (FSD&B). Thanks to New York State having enacted mandatory mainstreaming of children with disabilities, I was never sent to a segregated institution like FSD&B. Since Florida had no such requirement at the time, many disabled children in Florida were either sent to schools for the disabled or left in public schools with little or no support services.

The open house was heavily attended by busloads of high school students who filled the auditorium. I was struck by the number of blind youths in the audience who manifested rocking and other "blind-isms." I'd forgotten how prevalent such behaviors were. The program began with singing and musicianship by a group of blind students called Out of Sight.

In the second half of the program a troupe of deaf dancers performed to loud percussive music. One of the dancers was tall and strikingly beautiful. I turned to my companion, Carolyn, and commented, "She speaks and signs. I bet she'll be accepted into hearing society." At Lighthouse, I'd easily passed as sighted and was readily embraced by the White sighted staff. I had none of the blind mannerisms or malformed eye sockets that marked some of my fellow participants as disabled. Like me during my Lighthouse years, her "normal" looks and attractiveness could undoubtedly open doors in the same way.

If I'd been born a Floridian, I might have attended this very school and would not have had the wealth of experiences of mainstream schools like RHHS. Forced to attend New York public schools, I'd had to cope with being a small fish in a big pond. If I'd gone to upstate New York's School for the Blind in Batavia, I would have been a big fish in a very small pond. Of course, I did experience growing pains at leaving the insulated world of Lighthouse's recreation programs for the blind. But when the time came to join the world of the sighted, I was prepared to integrate thanks to my many years in mainstream schools.

Like this deaf performer at FSD&B, I was a good dancer, which helped make me more attractive to sighted women and men. It didn't hurt that I was a light-skinned Latino, unlike many of my fellow Black and Brown peers at Lighthouse. The combined advantages of my parents' gene pool, my social skills, and my lack of outward awkwardness all resulted in my way being eased.

But twenty-four hours after Carolyn and I visited FSD&B, I was abruptly reminded of my early roots. After bodysurfing at St. Augustine Beach, I tried to rinse off my contact lens only to have it blown away by the wind and lost in the sand. I always carry a spare contact, but the next day I felt a mild irritation in my one good eye. Carolyn inspected the replacement contact and noticed it was chipped. At that point, I had no extra contacts and my emergency eyeglasses were left back in Minnesota, where we lived. For the remainder of our vacation, I was forced to be extra careful to avoid losing my one link to normal eyesight in my good eye.

All this happened forty years after I'd undergone surgery to restore me to "normal" eyesight, and it was as if Spirit were reminding me of my old identity as a "Blink." Today's FSD&B students seemed little inclined to stage sit-ins or protest for greater independence and autonomy. Their White sighted teachers were well-intentioned enough but clearly ran the show. Watching the headmaster up on stage, he struck me as kind, but patronizing. Back at Lighthouse during our protest and sit-in, management was startled by our demands for greater self-determination as blind people in an institution run entirely by the sighted.

As I left the palm-tree-draped school grounds, I wondered what my life might have been like if I'd lived at FSD&B. Ray Charles was a graduate of the school back in 1941. I would have come home on weekends but lived at the school during the week. No participation in a mainstream high school swim team that eventually made it to the New York City semifinals, no presidency of the Ecology Club, no student vice presidency. No dating sighted girls. How fickle was Fate when a simple accident of birth and geography had so major a bearing on my life's course?

In the 1960s and 1970s, despite mainstreaming, New York State still ran the Batavia School for the Blind (and still does today), but many of its students were severely disabled. None of the kids I knew that went to Batavia went on to college; most became piano tuners, masseuses, or newspaper kiosk workers. The bar for me at Batavia would've been set considerably lower. My later life as a community organizer and university professor likely would have gone unrealized, my potential unfulfilled.

18.   Mugging on Friday the 13th, 1972

I'M SEVENTEEN AND SOUND ASLEEP when I hear the scream. Swimming up from a dream, I sit bolt upright up in bed. I roll over and see that the large red letters on the bedside clock read 2:03 a.m. I hear it again and understand this is no dream. A woman's voice clearly pleads, "Help! Help!"

It's a hot September night and we have no air-conditioning, so I'm sleeping buck naked. Tugging on my cutoff shorts, I grab the nine-inch bowie knife from under my mattress. Ever since the Hells Angels started selling drugs out of the used car lot up on Atlantic Avenue, the neighborhood has seemed a lot less safe. I dash down the hallway of our shotgun-style first-floor apartment and throw open the front door. All the houses on our block are packed tightly one on top of another and there are no lights on. I peer up the street, and then down. Nothing. Suddenly in the hushed stillness I hear faint scuffling sounds in the narrow alleyway two houses away. I know that Mrs. Puglisi, the mother of our swim-team captain, Mike, works the night shift as a nurse and lived there.

I yell, "Mrs. P, is that you?" in their direction. I just barely make out the shadow of a figure as it leans out from their alley. I hear another "Help me!" Barefoot, I run down our stoop toward their alley shouting, "Muthafucker, I got a knife, and I'm goin' to cut you up bad!"

Just then the Puglisis' front porch light comes on. In its pale-yellow glare, a short, scrawny White guy with a dark watch cap scrambles out of their alley and begins running towards Atlantic

Avenue. Looking nervously over his right shoulder, he dashes between two parked cars. In the shadows of the dimly lit street, he
quickly disappears from my sight. A second later, an ashen and di-
sheveled Mrs. P emerges from the alley clutching her handbag.

"Mrs. P, it's me, Jimmy Bonilla. You okay?"

Her groggy son Mike emerges from the front door, and I explain,
"I think a guy just tried to mug your mom."

"I'm okay, I'm okay," insists the shaking Mrs. P.

Mike takes her arm and, brushing the dirt off her white nurse's
uniform, slowly helps her up the brick stoop onto their covered
porch. Before she goes inside she turns to Mike and says, "Jimmy
scared that shit away. And I still have my purse!" She shakes the
purse overhead like a trophy. Mike and I crack up laughing and, a
moment later, so does Mrs. P.

Years afterward I wondered, beside teenage male bravado,
what motivates a person to leap into a dangerous situation to help
a neighbor? Growing up in Queens, I'd heard the story of the horrendous 1964 murder of a young woman named Kitty Genovese.
What turned the story into a national urban legend was that thirty-
eight neighbors supposedly heard her scream for help outside their
apartments that night but did nothing to intervene. The tale became symbolic of all that was wrong with New York City in particular, people in general, and the dehumanizing impact of cities. It gave
rise to countless studies on "the bystander effect" that purported to
prove people were apathetic and uncaring. It sold millions of papers
for the *New York Times* and fueled White fear of urban crime. It was
a horrifying story. There was only one problem. The story turned
out not to be true.

No one witnessed the actual attack. However, over the course
of thirty-five minutes, numerous neighbors called police after hearing screams. Despite the potential danger to herself, one neighbor,
Sophia Farrar, forced open a wedged door to the vestibule behind
their building, where the attack had taken place. She found Kitty
lying in a pool of blood, yelled for neighbors to call the police, and
cradled the bleeding woman until an ambulance arrived, whispering, "Help is on the way." This was how Kitty Genovese really died:
not ignored, not alone, but wrapped in her neighbor's arms. On that

fateful night, it wasn't human nature or the neighbors who failed Kitty. It was the authorities' failure to respond quickly.

The truth was eventually revealed fifty-five years later in the book *Humankind: A Hopeful History* by Rutger Bregman. But to one nine-year-old from Queens, the Genovese story had an enduring impact. It partially explained why eight years later I'd decide to rush to the aid of a fellow human being in the middle of the night.

That experience taught me a profound lesson on why it was critical to help neighbors and it helped lay the groundwork for my future vocation as a community organizer.

19.   "But You Don't Look..."

> Lightness ... is a lonely gift.
> —BRIT BENNETT, *THE VANISHING HALF*

GROWING UP I sometimes felt like an imposter, too sighted to be seen as blind, too light-skinned to be seen as Puerto Rican. This often left me feeling isolated and apart, not really belonging in either group. Because I was a "high partial" (a partially sighted person), I'd often be at the receiving end of comments like "But you don't look blind." What, I wondered, does a guy have to do to be accepted? Carry a cane? Have a seeing-eye dog? Read braille?

Unfortunately, this isn't an unusual experience among visually impaired people. The performer M. Leona Godin tells a story of an older blind gentleman who'd been sitting in the San Francisco BART station with his guide dog reading the newspaper. A stranger came up to him and said, "You don't look blind!" So the man reached into his bag, pulled out his dark sunglasses, put them on, and continued to read his paper. Likewise, being light-skinned I'd sometimes hear "But you don't look Puerto Rican." Less humorously, that comment occasionally carried a whiff of a supposed compliment. In those instances, my reply was a slightly snide "Oh really? Do you know a lot of Puerto Ricans?"

The idea that there is only one type of blind person, presumably a completely sightless one, is a myth not unlike the notion that one can tell if a person is Puerto Rican. Some people have been blind since birth, others have blindness come later in life. Some blind folks suffer from central vision loss while others lose their peripheral sight when their visual field narrows. There are blind folks, like me, who suffer from blurred vision and others who have visual disorders following brain injuries or accidents. Think of blindness as a continuum: from sighted to partially sighted to totally blind. The vast majority of blind people fall into an in-between category.

Like blindness, the color of skin among Puerto Ricans comes in many shades. There is racism in Puerto Rico, but it tends to be hidden and silent, with a history far different from that of the United States. Puertorriqueños have been U.S. citizens by birthright since 1917, and no laws on the island prohibited people of different shades from eating at the same restaurant, sleeping in the same hotel, or dating and marrying. Many talented ballplayers from the Negro leagues, banned from the major-league baseball in the United States, were hired to play for San Juan's teams and hailed as stars by Puerto Ricans of all ages and colors. The elites of San Juan tended to be White and boasted of their Spanish heritage, but being "a little dark" was not disqualifying. My great-grandmother was dark-skinned (morena), but it did not prevent her from becoming an education commissioner on the island.

Not unlike the Inuit people of the North, who reportedly have dozens of names for snow, Puerto Ricans have many terms to describe the nuances of race. Some of those terms include:

moreno—dark-skinned, assumed to be Black

prieto—Black, but of a lower class

piel oscura—dark-skinned

negrito—a "little" Black boy

trigueño elegante—an elegant Black person

mulatto—of Black and Spanish descent

café con leche—having the color of coffee with milk (like my dad)

jabao—high yellow

triste de color—sad color

indigenía—of Indigenous descent (like my mother's mother, Aurea)

Taíno—of the native people of Puerto Rico

trigueño—triracial (any mix of Taíno, Spanish, and African)

trigueño con pelo malo—might be mistaken for Indio if not for "bad hair"

mestizo—a mix of White and Taíno, Spanish, or African

chino—of Asian descent

rubia—blond or fair-skinned (like my mother)

blanco—a White person

blanquito—White person of the upper class

blanquito con pelo malo—might be mistaken for White if not for "bad" hair

Blanquito con pelo malo was sometimes used to describe me as a youngster when my hair was curlier and darker. Unlike in the United States, where race is implicitly linked to social class, race in Puerto Rico is explicitly linked to social class. There is a saying there that "money whitens." Although overt racism is not as prevalent as it is in the United States, it was not uncommon for grandparents to wish that a grandchild be born blanquita or blanquito. Another Puerto Rican saying goes "El que no tiene Dinga tiene Mandinga." Translated, it means nearly every Puerto Rican has some African ancestry. My mother's generation might speak quietly of "improving the race" by having offspring with someone of a lighter complexion. Curious as an adult, I sent away to have my genetic code tested using Ancestry.com. My results revealed that 60 percent of my DNA origins trace to the Iberian Peninsula, in Italy, Portugal, and Spain. Meanwhile, 20 percent of my DNA results include African and Taíno strands, bearing out the old adage.

Not unlike this view of race in Puerto Rico, among some in the larger blind community there is a silent hierarchy. Blind people who also are developmentally disabled can be shunned or seen as less than. But just as there has been coalition building across races, valuing some disabilities over others is slowing becoming more and more rare within the youth-driven disability justice movement.

20. "Dad, I Can't Play Golf."

Let us never forget that the fate of the blind community is
the fate of all minorities. At very best they are tolerated.
They are almost never understood.

—JACQUES LUSSEYRAN

WHEN I WAS ELEVEN my father took me to King of Prussia, Pennsylvania, to visit his Korean War buddy John Sr. My father rarely took me anywhere out of town on our weekend visitations, so this was a big deal. John Sr. had a family with two boys roughly my age. I was apprehensive at first, but they turned out to be kind and welcoming. Soon we were dashing around in their backyard, which seemed huge by Queens standards. Running alongside their backyard was a small creek.

John Jr. turned to me with a glint in his eye and said, "Wanna check out our muskrat traps? I learned how to make snares in Boy Scouts this summer." A city boy, I was clueless about muskrats and traps and didn't know what a muskrat or snare even looked like.

"Sure," I said. "Sounds cool!"

John Jr. and his little brother Harry took me down to the creek and they signaled me to hush as they slowly pulled on a string tied to a sapling that led underwater. Together, they carefully pulled the heavy trap out of the strong current. Slowly a shiny, limp, dark-brown body emerged. The brothers were so excited that Harry immediately ran to the house to tell their dad. Meanwhile, John Jr. dragged the motionless creature onto the grass and we proceeded to examine it. Its head was caught in a wire noose, but otherwise it seemed to be sleeping. I gently poked at it with a twig to be sure it was dead.

"When he takes the bait and puts his head in the noose it pulls tight. He can't come up for air and drowns," John Jr. explained.

John Sr. and Kiko returned shortly and my father said, "Wow, you snared a mink. Very valuable fur, but if you want to get money for the pelt you'll need to skin it yourselves." The boys and I simultaneously uttered a collective "Ugh." Kiko laughed at our squeamishness, but their father was insistent. "You took its life, and it's up to you not to waste it."

"Can't you do that, Dad?" John Jr. pleaded.

"When you asked permission to run a trap line, I told you you'd have to see it through. Just be careful you don't hit the scent gland when you're removing the pelt. A mink's spray smells as bad as a skunk's."

Leaving us to the work of skinning the mink, the two men returned to the house. Meanwhile John Jr. took out his penknife. Looking to me he said, "You wanna do it? I'll let you."

"Nah," I replied. "Don't want to mess it up for you. You go 'head. I'll watch."

Disappointed by my lack of expertise, or willingness, he hesitantly commenced removing the wire noose from the dead mink's neck. Gingerly, with his brother and me standing over him, he began to slice open the poor animal's belly. A mix of blood and guts spilled out, exposing purple entrails. We were totally grossed out but fascinated at the same time.

"I think once he's cut open I can peel his hide off in one piece," John Jr. said. The confidence in his voice left a bit to be desired. Near the bottom of the belly the knife must've cut too deeply and nicked the scent gland. Suddenly we were enveloped in a noxious cloud of mink stink. It was so foul my eyes burned and I was forced to turn away so I could catch my breath. Bearing the full brunt of the released stench, John Jr. was coughing, choking, and gagging all at the same time. He dropped his penknife and ran crying up to the house. His brother and I trailed behind him at a safe distance. And that's how I learned I didn't want to become a trapper when I grew up.

The day after the mink fiasco my dad and John Sr. decided to go golfing. Since his boys had gone off with their mother shopping for school clothes, John Sr. arranged for me to work at the driving range while he and my dad played a round. I was super excited and anxious all at once. At eleven years old, this would be my first paying job. And my father would get to watch me!

"You get paid for every ball you retrieve," John Sr. explained. It sounded simple enough to my eleven-year-old mind, but in the back of my brain there was a sense of foreboding. Perhaps the previous day's mayhem with the mink had colored my confidence.

Turning to Kiko, I said, "Dad, I can't play golf." Dismissing my concern out of hand, Kiko said, "You don't need to know golf. Watch those men up there," He pointed toward a line of men up a hill just barely within my line of sight. "When they hit the ball, all you have to do is go retrieve it. Easy as pie."

With that said, he and John Sr. climbed into their waiting golf cart and headed off, leaving me alone to face my first ball. The manager at the pro shop gave me a red plastic helmet like baseball players wear when they're at the plate. It was too big, and I was confused as to why I'd even need head protection. Embarrassed to ask, I went outside and stood alone at the bottom of the driving-range hill awaiting the arrival of my little flying paychecks.

There was only one problem. Although I could hear the sound of the men hitting the balls (SWACK, SWACK, SWACK), because of my limited sight I couldn't actually see them once they were airborne. White dimpled golf balls began landing all around me. Desperately, I clutched the basket and began to collect those white balls I could see against the green of the turf. Meanwhile, I kept hearing the SWACK, SWACK, SWACK sounds. After a bit, the men on top of the hill began shouting at me to get off the range. Puzzled, I didn't know whether to collect the balls I was seeing or retreat. To make matters worse, my father was nowhere in sight.

CRACK! Suddenly a ball ricocheted off my helmet and I quickly understood why they were yelling and why I was wearing the helmet. I was now in danger of being seriously hurt. I began to run in the opposite direction, but another ball took a wicked bounce and hit my calf. Yelping in pain and afraid of what was to come, I made a frantic retreat back to the pro shop.

In tears, I explained to the manager that I was legally blind and couldn't really see the balls until they were on the ground. Feelings of embarrassment, humiliation, and shame covered me like a smelly wet blanket.

Sensing my distress he said, "It's okay, it's okay. Just sit here and watch TV until your dad is done." I whiled away an hour watching a boring golf tournament. After my father and John Sr. returned, the manager explained why I wasn't out on the driving range. A former semipro athlete, my father seemed at a loss until the manager snorted, "Jesus, the kid can't see the balls coming at him. This is no kind of job for a blind boy." Seeing me bereft, the manager then did an amazing thing. Opening his cash register, he said, "Look, kid, I saw that at least you tried. And you took a couple of good hits out there, so here's twenty dollars for your effort."

Stunned, I took the crisp twenty-dollar bill and carefully folded it into the pocket of my blue Levi's jeans. I remember thinking, *At least my first job wasn't a total disaster.*

"Thanks, mister," I managed to mumble.

Choking back a sob, I turned to my John Sr. and my dad. "Sorry I didn't do better." So much for my father watching me. It was the first time I recognized he didn't understand his blind son's world, and it hit me hard. That day, my sense of distance from my father and subsequent feelings of isolation and loneliness because of my blindness only intensified.

21.   A Blind Messenger?

A FTER THE HUMILIATION of my first job at the driving range, I was afraid to test myself again. What if my second job turned out to prove my total incompetence for the world of work? Because I took services at New York's Lighthouse for the Blind, I knew too many blind people who lived in or near poverty thanks to limited job prospects. Was that where I was headed?

I got my chance at redemption at my mother's workplace, the *Long Island Press* newspaper, where she had an "in" with the advertising department. They needed messengers to take advertising copy into Manhattan from their Jamaica, Queens, headquarters. At sixteen, looking ahead at the expense of college, I was determined to prove I could earn money and not look the fool. But I also knew that messengers were required to navigate Manhattan and the dangers of 1970s New York City's subway system alone.

Before I could embark on this new adventure I had to meet Mr. Robeson, the dispatcher and head of messenger services for the *Press*. His office was in the grimy basement of the newspaper building. The stairwell down was filled with the odor of newspaper rolls and ink presses. Opening the basement's rusty, green metal door, I entered a small, dingy open space with four desks strewn randomly across the room. I asked the nearest messenger where I could find Mr. Robeson.

Mr. Robeson, a heavyset Black man in a chair, beckoned me toward his gunmetal-gray desk. It had three phone lines and an inbox and outbox for pending arrivals and deliveries. He looked to be in his sixties. He immediately welcomed me with a broad, kind smile. His eyes expressed a gentleness that was hard to miss, even for me. Since he hadn't stood, I took a chair alongside his desk. That's when I noticed the wheelchair and the small oxygen tank tucked away in the corner. Around his neck hung a slim blue hose with nose clips.

Noticing my gaze, Mr. Robeson said, "I have emphysema, so the fresh air helps me breathe easier." Pointing to the empty left cuff of his pants, he added, "Lost the leg to the Diabeteeze last year."

That's when I noticed his Southern accent. His was a deep baritone voice that immediately instilled confidence. So did the fact that here was a supervisor with a disability, and my first boss of color.

"So, James, how well do you know your way around the subways?" he asked.

I decided honesty would be the best policy, so I said, "Sir, I can take the train from here to home on Seventyfifth Avenue"—just five stops away—"but that's it."

A rumbling laugh erupted from deep inside his sizable belly. Chuckling, he said, "Not to worry, James. We'll get you up to speed in no time. After three weeks you'll be a master of the New York subway system."

I immediately liked Mr. Robeson. I later learned that the other messenger boys, most older than me, were totally devoted to him.

I started delivering ad copy to Manhattan advertising agencies in Midtown and quickly learned my way around the Big Apple. Thanks to Mr. Robeson's directions, and the fact that I got on a first-name basis with the token booth operators who I asked for help, I was soon giving friends and out-of-town tourists directions. Finally, a job where I felt accomplished!

One of my favorite aspects of this after-school job was that once I completed my initial round of deliveries I had to wait for the ad agencies to call Mr. Robeson for last-minute pickups. It was during one such break that I discovered Paley Park on Fifty-third Street in Midtown. It was the former site of the notorious Stork Club, a speakeasy made infamous during the 1930s Prohibition era. As an act of atonement, after the building was torn down, the lot was donated to the city as a park. The back wall farthest from the street had been fashioned into a three-story waterfall. Rows of locust trees were planted parallel to the sidewalls so that when one entered from the street, the waterfalls were perfectly framed by the twin rows of locusts. Black metal mesh tables and chairs were positioned under the trees, where I could casually sip a coffee I'd buy from the closet-sized concession stand at the street-side entrance.

The magic of Paley Park is that as a passerby steps inside, the sights and sounds of the city are blocked by the trees and drowned out by the soothing sound of the falling waters and chirping sparrows. I was intensely proud that, on my own, I'd discovered an oasis of Mother Earth in the midst of New York's hustle and bustle. Later, I'd relish sharing my "discovery" with friends and visitors.

Refreshed after my stopover, I'd continue my late pickups and eventually return to Jamaica on the express train, which I'd catch at Grand Central Station. I never tired of Grand Central's timeless and awe-inspiring architecture. A large plaque outside testified to the fact that it was on the National Register of Historic Places.

Back at the *Press*, Mr. Robeson was always there waiting. "So, James, no problems finding things I assume? Have a good day?" he'd ask.

"Yes, sir. I love Manhattan," I'd reply.

As well as the financial rewards of my first real job, I came to relish the mobility and independence the subway afforded me. The challenges as a legally blind kid learning my way around so huge a system only reinforced my deepening sense of resourcefulness and self-reliance. Each payday I'd make my way to the cash-and-carry loan agency on the corner and proudly watch while the woman behind the cage cashed my check and counted out my earnings. Soon the pain and shame of my Pennsylvania driving-range debacle became a distant memory.

22. Stigma

WHEN I WAS TEN we lived in a three-block area of Queens that had several five-story apartment buildings. Our neighborhood bully, Eddie, lived in one with his single mother. I had a run-in with Eddie once, when he knocked me off my bike to impress some neighborhood girls. To his and my surprise, I bounced off the pavement and came up swinging. He was five years older, a head taller, and about twenty-five pounds heavier than I was. Eddie must have found my feistiness amusing, but not so much that he didn't proceed to pin me to the ground, laughing at my stupidity. Eventually, the girls he was trying to impress took pity on me and shamed him into letting me go. From that day onward I gave Eddie a wide berth.

A few months later while getting off the school bus, I noticed a crowd of local kids amassing in front of Eddie's building. Looking up, I could just see Eddie's mother sitting on the inside ledge of their fourth-floor apartment's picture window, smoking a cigarette. She looked like she was just getting some rays, a ritual she did often on that same ledge. Except today, I was told by a friend, she was topless. Her long red hair did little to conceal her ample breasts from the gawking eyes of the neighborhood kids.

Eddie was positioned under the window, looking up and yelling, "Ma, please go inside. Please Ma! Ma!" But his pleas had no impact. His mom just laughed and continued to languidly puff on her cigarette like an old-time movie starlet.

Standing in the gathering crowd, I asked a kid I knew from the building, "What's up with Eddie's mother?"

"My mom says she gets pretty drunk during the day and she's been off her meds for a while," he replied.

Confused, I asked, "Meds? For what?"

The kid raised his right hand and with his index finger next to his right temple, did a circular, whirling motion. Perhaps fearing Eddie might overhear, he nervously whispered, "She's nutso, man. Everyone knows she's out of her head. A total wacko."

We both became uncomfortable, and not because Eddie's mom was half-naked. Staring up at the spectacle that was his mother, Eddie was openly crying in front of everyone. Not just a sniffle or two, but deep, racking sobs. The kid everyone had been terrified of was having a meltdown in front of our eyes. It was the first time anyone I knew had been singled out publicly as being mentally ill.

Normally a child would tell a parent about something like this, but strangely, that night I avoided telling my mom what happened. Later in bed, reliving Eddie's pain and humiliation, I suppressed an urge to vomit. While I could summon up little empathy for Eddie's mom, I definitely related to Eddie's hidden pain and shame. If they hadn't before, now everyone in the neighborhood would know his mother was mentally ill.

* * *

As I was nearing graduation with a bachelor's degree in therapeutic recreation, the country was in the midst of a deep recession, and I wondered if I'd ever be able to find a job in my field. As my good luck would have it, the previous fall, one of my professors at SUNY Cortland talked me into taking the New York State Civil Service exam for recreation therapists. It had taken months, but one sunny afternoon the following May I came home to my shared off-campus apartment to find an official looking envelope from the State of New York. Inside was a letter from the State Civil Service Commission congratulating me on passing the exam:

Given your excellent score on the exam, you are hereby offered the position of Recreation Therapist, Grade II at Creedmoor Psychiatric Center in Queens, New York. Your starting
salary will be $37,000 a year and you will be entitled to full
health coverage, life insurance and retirement benefits.

Standing in our little student apartment, you could have knocked
me over with a feather boa. Creedmoor? Growing up in Queens,
all I'd ever heard was that Creedmoor was the "Funny Farm," "the
Loony Bin," the place where they locked up people in padded cells.

It should have been a no-brainer. Up to that point, I'd worked
with many different kinds of disabilities: people with cerebral palsy,
strokes, MS, epilepsy, developmental disabilities, the blind, and
spina bifida. Never people who were primarily mentally ill. This
was a golden opportunity to expand my résumé by working with a
new population and get paid handsomely for it. Back in 1975, even
without all the benefits, thirty-seven thousand dollars was a huge
salary in the field. The other positions I'd been exploring had sala-
ries starting at eighteen thousand or twenty-two thousand dollars a
year and didn't come close to matching New York State's generous
benefits package. When my classmates in the program found out
about the offer, they were green with envy.

But I knew from the get-go that I wasn't going to take the job.
Several days later, laughing uncomfortably over dinner, I told my
roommate, "No way I'm going to work with the crazies. They're
way too unpredictable. They're dangerous." This was ironic, coming from a kid who'd grown up with a mother who'd struggled with
mental illness.

My roommate was dumbfounded. "You're going to turn down
all that money? In the middle of a recession?"

"They couldn't pay me enough!" I said.

I never gave the position a second thought because like so many
others, I'd absorbed all the negative stereotypes about people with
mental illness. The image of Eddie's mother on the ledge, nearly
naked as a jaybird, was permanently etched into my memory, as was
the image of big, bad Eddie weeping uncontrollably. Unconsciously,
I'd completely bought into the stigma of the mentally ill as "nutsos,"

"loonies," "off their rockers," and "total whack jobs." I wasn't prepared to deal with my fears nor confront my stereotypes head on.

Looking back, I now understand that mental illness was not just
something I'd seen on TV. It was something I lived with my entire
childhood. It was the reason I never discussed my mother's erratic
behavior with anyone growing up, not even with my father during
his infrequent weekend visitations.

Already having been stereotyped for being blind and Puerto
Rican, I didn't want to be associated and stereotyped with the mentally ill. I was repelled by the idea that someone might know that
my mother was wacko. From Eddie, I'd learned of the dreaded humiliation that label would bring down not just on our mothers, but
on me.

"Those people scare me shitless," I confessed to my roomie. But
what I was really afraid of was my mother, and that the stigma of
Dee being labeled wacko might eventually rub off on me.

I was already having to cope with the complexity of being a disabled, light-skinned Puerto Rican in America. I turned down that
plum job at Creedmoor Psychiatric Center because I'd developed a
"blind spot" about mental illness I wasn't prepared to acknowledge,
even when I came face to face with it. But come face to face with it
I did.

23. Titi Anna

I T'S AN OLD SAW that everyone has a "crazy" aunt or uncle some-where in their family closet, but no one talks about it.

Titi Anna was the tallest of my father's sisters. Standing nearly six feet tall with hair as black as midnight, she exuded a stately bearing. Well educated, refined, and handsome in a way that calls forth images of a young Sigourney Weaver, Anna was a stunning beauty. In a sepia photograph from the 1950s, she wears a formal black gown and is surrounded by dashing young naval officers in white uniforms. The photograph was taken at an embassy reception and dance at the Waldorf Astoria Hotel welcoming the Argentine fleet to New York. She was also the Anna responsible for introducing her younger brother, my father, to my mother.

After I was born and it was discovered that I couldn't see out of my left eye, Anna approached my father and mother to say that she wanted to donate one of her eyes to me. Although it turned out that wasn't a solution for my eye condition, it was how I came to appreciate her unconditional love for her nephew.

My mother was fond of saying "No one was ever good enough for Anna." In fact, Anna was the only one of my father's three sisters who was referred to as "the spinster aunt." She lived with my grandmother until Anna was in her midfifties. Eventually, she settled for what Dee described as a loveless marriage to a German engineer named George. George was a taciturn, rich, older man who collected classic flamenco recordings. My impression of him was that he was as aloof and detached as the money he seemed to worship. My father detested George, both because he didn't show Anna sufficient devotion and because he was miserly to a fault. I recall going out to a seafood restaurant in Freeport with my father, Anna, and George. When the check came, George excused himself and went to the restroom. He was gone a very long time. As my father paid the check, he leaned over to me and said, "The son of a bitch always pulls this crap."

When I was a child, Anna delighted in picking me up from my crib and dancing around Nana's apartment with me in her arms. I know from my mother that George never took Anna dancing.

A few years into their marriage and soon after Nana's death, Anna landed in the psych unit at Bellevue Hospital in Manhattan. I was only fourteen and was not allowed to go upstairs and visit the locked ward, so I waited outside on First Avenue while my father went in. Honestly, I was relieved not to have to go into the scary-looking place. He reappeared soon and took me around the corner of the huge Gothic citadel to the Twenty-seventh Street side, saying, "Anna wants to see you." Once we were in position, I spotted her feebly waving at me through the barred window of her shared third-floor room. Even at fourteen, I knew something was off.

When I asked why she was in the hospital, my father said, "She's struggling with Nana's death and is having some emotional problems. Who wouldn't, being married to the Jerk?" (His pet name for George.) "But seeing you always makes her happier." After several weeks in the hospital, Anna was released back into George's care, but she spent the remainder of her life in a drug-induced fog. When I'd visit, I'd watch, horrified, as she robotically walked across her living-room carpet, stiff-legged and zombie-like. At times the expression on her face seemed vacant, and at other times angry. I found myself a little afraid to be alone with her. Then I'd say something goofy or tell her a story, and the old Anna would reemerge. She'd laugh aloud and a familiar sparkle would come back into her eyes, only to quickly fade away, replaced by a thousand-yard stare.

In my junior year in college, I got an unexpected call from my father. "Anna is very sick, and she would love to see you. Could you get free to come down here? I'll spring for the bus fare." Although the tone of his voice seemed nonchalant, I knew it had taken a great deal for him to reach out and ask. The next morning, I took the Greyhound bus from Cortland in upstate New York to the Port Authority, where my father picked me up. In the car he growled, "The Jerk is so fucking cheap he won't even spring for a private room."

When we arrived at the hospital Anna's door was closed. Annoyed, my father knocked loudly. From inside Anna's voice weakly asked, "Please don't come in yet." Undeterred, upon hearing George's voice in the room my father burst in. From the doorway I could see that poor Anna was lying amid soiled bedclothes. A Jamaican nurse's aide was gently wiping her bottom.

Politely, the aide said, "We'll be finished here in a minute, gentlemen. Perhaps it's better if you wait outside."

The fecal stench in the room was overpowering, and my father and I quickly retreated back into the hallway. I was simultaneously embarrassed for Anna and furious that I might be associated with my father's thoughtless impatience. After a few long moments, the aide came out and gave my father a cross look, but to me she smiled and said, "It's okay to go in now, hon."

Anna was in fresh pajamas, and as soon as I entered the room her broad, shiny face broke into a wide smile. "Jimmy, you've come so far just to see me? I love that you did that," she said. She then began to cry softly. I stepped over and gave her a buss on the cheek, which seemed to help her regain her composure. As we left the hospital, my father finally disclosed, "It's rectal cancer, and the prognosis is very bad."

On the return trip, sitting alone on the Greyhound bus, I gazed out at the setting sun as we passed the darkening woods and pastures of central New York state. I'd hoped that my presence perhaps lightened her Spirit. Three days later my father called to say that Anna had died that night. It was the only time I'd ever heard an emotional catch in his voice.

My father would never speak again about what caused Anna to be institutionalized in Bellevue or remain on such strong drugs that she was barely functional. Not unlike my mother's mysterious "three-week vacation," neither side of our family ever breathed the words "mental illness." That left me with no one to confide my own struggles to back at college.

24. Clark Tower

A FTER YEARS OF THERAPY for my own struggles with depression and anxiety, I experienced a breakthrough in my fifties. It came to me in the guise of a recurring dream I'd had since childhood, a nightmare starring me as a five-year-old.

In the dream, I'm back in our little apartment in Forest Hills. At the center of the apartment is a small hallway that connects the living room, bathroom, bedroom, and kitchen. In the center of this small hallway a yawning chasm has opened up. To a five-year-old it seems a gigantic, bottomless black hole. Defying gravity, I manage to peddle my tricycle around the narrow periphery of the large abyss while magically avoiding falling in. I can't see or hear her, but I sense that my mother has somehow fallen in and has been swallowed into the hole's darkness.

"Mamí, Mamí, where are you?" I call out. "Please come out. Mamí, Mamí!" But in my dream my cries echo against the walls with no response. In the stark white emptiness of the apartment, I'm hungry and feeling alone and abandoned.

My therapist explained that even as a five-year-old, I'd intuited that my mother had fallen into a metaphorical pit fueled by her anxiety and depression. The dream was my way of signaling the depth and fear of my own loneliness and feelings of abandonment. First there was her as a child of fourteen, witnessing the horrendous death of her mother. This was followed by her estrangement from her father and, later, her first love, the young doctor. Years later came her divorce from my father, and then the home robbery. All her previous traumas were rekindled by the break-in and caused her posttraumatic stress disorder (PTSD) to erupt at erratic intervals.

Research has begun to show that parents can pass on their anxiety and depression to their offspring through their genes. Several therapists tell me that the origins of my depression are likely connected to the effects of my mother's PTSD. Their guess is that her episodes of harsh and cruel behavior toward me were partly triggered by her PTSD. The consequences of that genetic hand-me-down were about to reveal themselves.

*   *   *

Clark Tower is one of Cortland State 's four ten-story residence halls. Its top floor offers a beautiful vista of the town's water reservoir and surrounding forest. The reservoir's trees glow in vivid shades of gold, orange, and red. I turn and glance anxiously behind me to the sterile, shadowy stairwell. Staring down ten stories and perched precariously on the open windowsill, I feel my legs begin to shake. If someone comes up the stairs, I'll have to quickly climb down, or rush my leap before I'm ready . . .

*   *   *

I'd been excited about going to college, the first in my family to attend. Cortland was a central New York state town renowned for the Cortland apple that grew on its lush, rolling hillsides. SUNY College at Cortland sat atop a hill overlooking the entire town. Ever since my drama with Dee over my Camp Lighthouse emancipation, I'd been looking forward to the escape from her that college would offer me. But it didn't take long to realize that, as one of only fourteen students of color on a campus of five thousand, maybe Cortland hadn't been the greatest choice.

Being mostly from the White suburbs of Long Island, my dormmates were partial to mocking my preference for soul and salsa music, calling it "ghetto noise." I played Tito Puente, James Brown, and the Stylistics. They blasted Frank Zappa, the Who, and Uriah

Heep. They'd express their ethnocentrism by turning up their expensive stereos so it became difficult for me to think or study or hear my own music. My first three semesters in the dorm, I was routinely referred to as "Go-Go Gomez" (a racist 1960s TV cartoon character) or asked "Where's your switchblade, bro?" After going through three roommates, in my sophomore year I would end up in a single room, which only deepened my feelings of isolation.

Like many first-year college students, I suffered from the usual teenage angst of separation from friends coupled with my first serious relationship breakup. Failing to make new friends deepened my darkening mood further. I was separated not only from my blind community at Lighthouse, but also from my friends of color and my estranged family. I became overwhelmed and felt awash in a sea of hostile, White middle-class culture. The sense of going under began to set in.

In my senior year, a female friend confided her puzzlement over why I'd ignored her friendly overtures two years earlier. The problem was I couldn't see her waving at me from across campus or in huge lecture halls. For me at the time, the campus beyond twenty feet was a blur. She'd thought me stuck up and hadn't known I was legally blind. "I thought blind people were totally blind," she confessed.

I, in turn, felt unseen, isolated, and deeply lonely. In Frank Bruni's memoir about slowly losing his sight, *The Beauty of Dusk,* he writes, "People with good vision underestimate the solace of the company of faces. You make eye contact. You read expressions. You communicate, you connect just by seeing. It's a lonely world, this one of not seeing."

Typical of my situation would be my freshman "Intro to Biology" seminar, which was held in a cavernous lecture hall filled with ninety students. The first two weeks of class, I'd raise my hand with a question only to be seemingly ignored by the professor. As my unanswered questions piled up, I began losing interest. One Friday afternoon at the end of class, this professor approached me as I packed up my knapsack. On weekends most kids could go home. That option was fraught for me, so weekends became my least favorite part of the semester.

"I'm wondering why you raise your hand, but then don't say anything when I point at you?" he asked. I explained that because I was legally blind, I didn't know he was acknowledging me unless he called me by name. A kind man, he shook his head in disbelief. "Could I be any more clueless! I'm terrible at learning names, but how about you sit in front and I start calling you Redcap?"

My preferred headwear that semester was a bright red watch cap I gotten to ward off the chilly fall air of upstate New York. From that day forward I'd be addressed with "Redcap, you have a question?" That professor later became a mentor who would recruit me for weekend biology field trips sponsored by the local chapter of the Izaak Walton League. Unfortunately, my other classes were not as accommodating, which only intensified my belief that not only was I without friends or family, but maybe I wasn't cut out for college. The death of Aunt Anna further exacerbated my depression to the point that I was drinking to excess, routinely oversleeping, and finding myself on the edge of ending my misery.

*   *   *

A stiff breeze blows red maple leaves across Clark Tower's browning lawn below. It's late afternoon and the setting sun is creating thermals. As I gaze out over what I believe may be my last look at the hills of Cortland, I feel torn between dueling impulses: to climb down from the prospect of a painful end or stop the misery of my lonely existence. Gripping the window rails, I notice my palms have become sweaty. A shadow suddenly passes over me. Startled, I look up. I see a red-tailed hawk floating so close by that I think I could almost reach out and touch its outstretched wings. As it banks, the scarlet sun catches the crimson of its tail feathers and they burn vividly against the clear blue October sky. It seems the universe is flashing me a bright red STOP sign.

As night falls I return to my single room, emotionally exhausted. I collapse onto my bed fully clothed and sleep for the next sixteen hours, but it is a restless sleep. The next day is Saturday, and I awake feeling still tired, but curiously optimistic. It is a glorious autumn day, and with no destination in mind I decide to take my bike out for a ride. After about two hours I'm well away from town, not quite lost, but not sure either of where I am exactly.

To my left I spy the silhouette of a lone tree atop a hill surrounded by empty farm fields and decide to rest. Dismounting, I push my bike uphill and across the empty field to rest under the bright yellow and orange canopy of this Old Oak. Its trunk is at least ten feet around and serves as a perfect backrest. Seated on the dry grass, I scan the panorama below us. In the distance is a farm with a fading red barn and a newer-looking dark blue and white silo. Farther west, just barely within my scope of vision, I see what looks like an orchard, neat rows of well-kept trees dotting the hillside. The famous Cortland apples.

White stratocumulus clouds scuttle quickly across the sapphire sky. Having survived my visit to Clark Tower, I'm feeling euphoric. My mood lifted, I feel connected to this spot, and grateful for the beauty surrounding me. It's as if the Old Oak sensed my loneliness and beckoned me over for a breather under its immense branches.

My eyes grow leaden as the events of the previous twenty-four hours, combined with my poor sleep and the long, hilly bike ride, conspire to make me drowsy. No longer feeling alone and glad to be alive, in no time I'm fast asleep. When I next awake, hours have passed and the temperature has dropped precipitously. The late-afternoon sky has turned a rose-tinged gray and the horizon is highlighted by streaks of orange and pink. Arising, I feel completely refreshed and thank my friend the Old Oak for its hospitality and take my leave. Giddily, I ride my bouncing bike down the steep hill back to the paved road. Retracing my route, I find my way back to the dorm just as the campus streetlights are blinking on.

25. "Oh, So Much Shame!"

I MET MY SOULMATE, Carolyn, when we were both in our early thirties and taking a university class on institutional racism. As a White girl raised for a time on the Nez Perce reservation in Idaho and the daughter of a disabled father, she was examining her experiences with White privilege, racism, sexism, and ableism. Recently, I confessed to her that I'd carried shame about being disabled, and Carolyn was stunned.

"In all our thirty-five years together, I've never heard you express shame about being blind, not once," she said.

Oh, I thought, *so much shame!*

It was decades before I fully comprehended what had driven me to the top of Clark Tower in 1973. Put in a word, the driver was a thing called shame. I'd spent part of my formative years in the predominately Jewish enclave of Forest Hills while attending a Catholic parochial school. It was no surprise that, thanks to my babysitter Mrs. Hirsch, who was Jewish, and the nuns at Our Lady Queen of Martyrs, feelings of shame and guilt were a cultural norm and a standard part of my upbringing.

Oh, so much shame:

Shame for not being able to recognize the faces of close friends or acknowledge people being friendly and just waving hello to me.

Shame at being perceived as just another blind man who

society pigeonholed as a nonsexual being, a neutered version of a "real" man, a curiosity without sexual appeal.

Shame for overcompensating by exaggerating my sexuality and becoming a stereotypical "Don Juan," a "Latin lover," or, as one astute female friend observed, a "traveling salesman" cliché.

Shame at only being visually impaired, and not being blind enough.

Shame at knowing how my disability must have disappointed my semipro baseball-playing father by not seeing well enough to play catch with him. Shame for not being a good enough son.

But my shame was unfortunately not limited to being visually impaired:

Shame at being a light-skinned Puerto Rican who could pass as White and not being seen as Puerto Rican enough.

Shame at being cast down into the "slow class" at Our Lady Queen of Martyrs, at not being perceived as smart enough.

After being banned from speaking Spanish by the nuns, shame at not being fluent in the language of my ancestors. Shame at not being Latino enough.

Shame at hearing my mother regularly liken me to my "lazy, irresponsible, ungrateful father." At not being a good enough son in her eyes either.

In *Harper's Magazine* Vivian Gornick observed humiliation, like shame, "can linger in the heart, the veins, the arteries forever, often deforming one's inner life." Like many, I've used the terms shame and guilt interchangeably. But I became curious about what exactly shame was, and how it was different from guilt.

Guilt, I learned, is the feeling that you did something wrong.

Shame, on the other hand, is the sense that your Whole Self is wrong, and it may not be related to any specific behavior or event. Typically, shame includes feelings that you are bad, worthy of contempt, inadequate, and unlovable.

Thankfully, with guilt you can take steps to atone and put your actions behind you. But feeling shame, being convinced you are the thing that's wrong, offers no clear-cut path to feeling more positive about yourself. It's as if shame is an emotional glue trap. In *Atlas of the Heart* Brené Brown writes, "the less we talk of shame, the more control it has over us. Shame hates being spoken." It thrives when kept hidden in the shadows. Small wonder that I'd never spoken to my wife or anyone else about my shame.

People who grow up in abusive environments can easily get the message they are inadequate, undeserving, and inferior. They're made to feel as if they should feel shame. The underlying fear that lay just under the surface of my shame was that I was destined for abandonment. The most extreme experiences of shame can become a form of self-annihilation. Shame was the thing that drove me to the top of Clark Tower.

But shame can also be a force for good. In *Harper's,* Gornick writes, "Shame can be salutary, shaking someone out of solipsism and complacency." In *Swing Time,* Zadie Smith observes, "Shame gets a bad rap. I think it can be a useful emotion, a corrective to certain kinds of behavior."

In *The Shame Machine,* Cathy O'Neil explains that one form of shame involves "punching down," deriding and shunning oneself or others, people who were shaped by forces beyond their control. For example, shaming others based on poverty, addiction, weight, race, or disability. But O'Neil believes that shame can alternatively involve "punching up."

As a young, disabled Puerto Rican, I eventually learned to discharge my shame by "punching up" against the powerful and the insensitive on behalf of those less empowered. Thanks to my involvement in the early disability rights movement, I began to transform my shame—my internalized ableism—into empathy and concrete social action. I discovered that I needn't be bitter and resentful. I needn't become someone who inflicts shame on myself or others. This releasing of my shame via empathy ultimately proved healthy and freeing. My earlier shame became fuel for positive change. By learning to let go of shame I would eventually be propelled into a life of social activism. But that was only to come later. Meanwhile, back at college I struggled mightily to belong and to develop compassion for myself and for others. It would take a drastic change of scenery for me to find my niche.

*   *   *

A week after I stood atop Clark Tower teetering on my heels, I ate dinner by myself as usual at my assigned dining hall. Afterward, I trudged to the student union for the weekly campus movie screening. Cortland usually had first-run feature movies, and the auditorium that night was three-quarters full. I don't recall what was shown, only that I sat there in a funk. After the movie, as I was leaving the union, I came upon a bright red flier pinned to the bulletin board in the lobby. Normally, I was unable to read campus flyers because they were in too small a print for me, but this one was in large, bold handwritten letters. It read:

Struggling to fit into campus life?
Want to meet new and interesting people?
Come to the first meeting of the CSU Rap Group.
This Friday at 7 PM,
CSU second floor lounge.

Like many firsts for me in college, I'd never been in a rap group, and I was suddenly curious. So, I went. During weekly meetings we'd do "check-ins" and usually have some sort of activity for getting to know one another, some of which were hokey, some interesting. The rap group was where I first recognized that I enjoyed being in small groups. I met two other students of color who shared similar frustrations to mine about being a minority on campus. It was where I also made my first real friend at Cortland. Facilitated by two second-year psych department grad students, the rap group broke through the isolation I'd been trapped in for nearly a year and a half. A month after my visit to the tower, I accidentally stumbled on a plan of escape from the drudgery of my campus life—one that did not involve taking my life.

One of my outdoor education professors was an older female pioneer in the field and a colorful character. Her reputation included a tale from her time at Wellesley College in Boston as an undergraduate. As a first-year from the hills of West Virginia, she'd smuggled her squirrel gun into her dormitory. One night, after one too many "brewskis" and a dare, she shot the rooster off the administration building's weather vane with a single shot from her dormitory window. From that night forward Marsha Carlson was nicknamed "Annie Oakley." Forty years later, the moniker had followed Professor Carlson to Cortland.

Marsha, a senior professor who ran Cortland's Outdoor Education Program, had been assigned as my official advisor. Before graduating from Cortland I'd be required to enroll in an outdoor practicum that entailed a three-week canoe and camping adventure in the Raquette chain of lakes in New York's Adirondack Mountains. For a Nuyorican city boy, it would profoundly influence how I'd come to embrace my life-long relationship to the natural world.

When I entered Professor Carlson's office for our first meeting, she immediately handed me a dog leash and ordered me to take Tango for a walk. Tango was her fourteen-year-old black-and-white cocker spaniel, a sweet but very overweight pooch. Our Recreation Department was in the newest building on campus, and huge signs at the entrances loudly declared NO PETS PERMITTED INSIDE. After Tango and I made several leisurely loops around the building, I returned and Professor Carlson finally sat me down next to her desk. As I was to learn was typical of her manner, she came directly to the point, without any of the usual preliminary niceties.

"We're beginning a new international program in Leisure Studies in England next semester. It will be at the Polytechnic of North London, and I think you'd be a good candidate." I'd already heard the announcement in other classes, but I'd dismissed the idea because it was only open to juniors and seniors and I was a lowly first-semester sophomore. Motioning with her arms for emphasis, she waved my reservation aside. "I'm the most senior professor in this damn department, and if I say you can go, that'll be that."

That's how I found myself on a red-eye to Heathrow on New Year's Eve 1973. Leaving JFK International Airport, I was headed away from racist undergrads, Clark Tower, and Dee, and toward a life-altering semester in London.

26. Learning Grace from Mrs. Reed

THE YEAR 1974 stood out for me. Among other things, Nixon resigned his presidency, Ali fought Foreman in the "Rumble in the Jungle," and Barbra Streisand had the top song of the year with "The Way We Were." Also, that summer I was forced to leave England when my eyesight worsened.

Our study-abroad semester was drawing to an end, and I'd landed a prestigious summer job at an adventure playground. Adventure playgrounds were the cutting edge of the new Adventure Playground movement of the 1970s, and this one was in London's Chelsea neighborhood—a cool, hip job in a cool, hip place.

Earlier that spring, I'd noticed my eyesight dimming, and then the British health services eye specialist confirmed the worst. The cataract in my one good eye had thickened dramatically, to the point that supervising children would be unwise. My night vision and ability to recognize faces diminished to the point that I was reduced to trying to recognize voices before I could make out who people were visually.

Crestfallen at having to leave England, I returned to New York City, where I stayed for two stressful weeks with Dee and her new husband John. Fortunately, Paul, one of my London friends, had returned to Cortland and invited me to live with him that summer. Confronting the prospect of a long, hot July and August in New York City with Dee, I immediately took him up on his offer.

Paul was holding down two jobs, one as a lifeguard and the second working at the Cortland Nursing Home (CNH). The nursing

Me, nineteen years old.

home was hiring, and I was soon riding my bike the five miles to do a night shift as an orderly. My job consisted mainly of assisting folks as they returned from dinner to get ready for bed. Most folks at CNH were in bed by eight, 8:30 p.m. at the latest. I was surprised at how little squeamishness I experienced emptying bedpans and helping elderly residents get undressed. Many proved grateful, and since I was the only male in our wing, the older ladies seemed to relish my attention. The all-female staff, mainly nurse's aides, were not only welcoming but flirtatious in an innocent way. Since it was always the same twenty or thirty residents going to the same rooms, I quickly learned to recognize their voices. My overall playful energy and ability to lift heavier residents more than compensated for my limited eyesight.

After helping folks into bed, we'd turn down our wing's hallway lights, and by 9:30 p.m. things would become very quiet. One nurse was a young woman named Debbie. Over coffee we'd get to talking at the nurse's station and she'd orient me to the various characters who inhabited our wing. Debbie was about five years my senior and resembled Michelle Pfeiffer, minus the glamor.

My most challenging resident was a very old gentleman named George. George had come to CNH after he suffered a major stroke that left him partially paralyzed and unable to speak. He rarely got visitors and did not seem to welcome or like any of the staff. Sadly, George routinely became so severely constipated that he required a staff person to help him evacuate his bowels. Debbie tutored me in the finer points of the procedure so as not to hurt him, but nevertheless he always became agitated. Since George also resisted letting staff trim his fingernails, his were long and sharp as razors. He seemed to take perverse delight in digging those nails into the arm of whatever unfortunate staff person was assigned to him. He was my least favorite resident because George fought back.

"Damn, George, cut that out!" I'd mutter.

After being left with a bleeding forearm more than once, I developed some insight into why some staff at other facilities might be accused of elder abuse. Debbie seemed to sense my annoyance. As she bandaged my bleeding forearm in the coffee lounge, I vented my frustration to her.

Debbie replied, "Imagine if you were left with no family to visit you. You can't speak, can't walk, and then on top of that, you suffer the physical pain of being so constipated it impacts your bowels."

There was no one else in the staff lounge at that moment. As I refilled my coffee cup, Debbie continued. "It can't do a lot for a person's dignity to have a stranger sticking a lubricated, gloved finger up your bare butt. I think George's scratching is his way of saying, 'Oh yeah, fella? Well, I'm still alive enough to fight!'" That night I learned an important lesson about compassion.

Going forward I made it a point to apologize to George beforehand, and I'd perform the uncomfortable procedure as quickly and gently as possible. George still scratched, but I learned not to take it personally.

The resident of CNH I recall most vividly was the elegant Mrs. Reed. She had one of only two private rooms in the entire facility, and it was liberally decorated with framed photographs of her husband as well as young people from all over the world. Unlike many residents, who spent their entire day clad in bathrobes and baggy pajamas, Mrs. Reed always came to dinner wearing a clean blouse, fashionable slacks, and a string of pearls with matching earrings. She didn't act superior to others; she was just well put together and always had a kind word for staff.

Unfortunately, Mrs. Reed suffered from rectal cancer, which in 1974 was often fatal, as it had been for Titi Anna. Unlike many of the female residents who seemed to relish having a man get them ready for bed, Mrs. Reed preferred a female. "James," she'd say, "a lady has to keep her dignity about her at all times, even if she is dying."

She often stayed up late into the night reading, her bedside lamp being the only illumination in the otherwise darkened room. When I'd notice her light on, if I wasn't too busy, I'd gently knock on her partially open door to check in on her. This was a routine we both came to appreciate. I'd pull up a chair and we'd talk. She'd been a high school teacher and happily married for forty years to a man she adored. The day of his retirement (he'd worked as a truck mechanic his entire life), he came home, walked up to their front door, and promptly dropped dead from a massive heart attack.

"I never thought I'd survive that," she said. Pausing to inhale, she continued, "But I had school and my students, and thanks to them, I made it through, one day at a time. I worked well past retirement age, until this damn cancer wouldn't let me."

It would be the one and only time I ever heard Mrs. Reed curse. Mrs. Reed had no children of her own, so she seemed to savor stories of my adventures in Europe. She'd also loved traveling, and one of her and her husband's favorite destinations was San Francisco. When I confessed I'd never been, she made me promise I'd go one day. It was mainly due to her enthusiasm that I'd choose San Francisco as my internship site the following summer.

As the fall set in, darkness came earlier and earlier, and riding my bicycle at night became trickier for me. Once or twice, as I'd pedaled home, the dark road would take an unexpected turn and I'd end up ass over teakettle, lying in the bottom of a roadside ditch. Thanks to the resilience of a young man's body, I never suffered more than a scraped knee or elbow and a bruised ego. But I began to wonder if the check from CNH was worth the risk of riding in the darkness, trying not to be run over or breaking my neck.

During this period, Mrs. Reed was suffering a great deal from her worsening cancer. After many weeks, she finally allowed me to help clean her up when a bout of diarrhea would come on her in the middle of the night. Embarrassed, she'd say, "Old age can be very hard. I'm sorry to burden you with this." Oddly, taking care of her even under those conditions didn't faze me.

"I consider it an honor that you let me be of service," I said. She simply smiled and nodded.

As her cancer progressed, her stools became more and more bloody, and her abdominal pain increased exponentially. Her fatigue and pain meds resulted in her often turning in early, and our conversations became fewer and further in between. Even as the cancer spread throughout her body, and despite her suffering, Mrs. Reed continued to dress for dinner until the week of Thanksgiving. By then she could no longer get out of bed, but whenever time allowed, I'd stop in and read short passages to her from whatever book she had on her night table, using my magnifying "Coke bottle" glasses.

On a cold winter's night in early December, I clocked in for my night shift and found Debbie crying softly in the staff coffee room. We were both close to Mrs. Reed and we'd both sensed the end was near. Debbie looked up through her tears to tell me she had died quietly earlier that morning. The rest of our shift passed uneventfully, but one could sense that even the residents with dementia understood something had happened, even if they hadn't heard that Mrs. Reed had left us.

As our shift ended, it began to snow heavily and Debbie offered me a ride home. She wasn't quite ready to go home, she said, so we had tea and Entenmann's coffee cake sitting next to one another at the kitchen table in my cramped student apartment. Debbie, who was married with two children, lingered over a second cup of tea. I began to wonder if our mutual attraction and shared grief might lead to something unexpected. Gazing at me, she finally said, "I better go home. Mrs. Reed would prefer it that way." I was disappointed, but also a bit relieved, as we hugged good night and she left.

My fall semester ended shortly, and after Christmas break I gave notice and never returned to CNH. But the kindness and spirit of Mrs. Reed in the face of death never left me. The following summer, in 1975, I began my college internship at San Francisco's Janet Pomeroy Recreation Center for the Handicapped. One night I was sitting with friends at a window booth at the famous Buena Vista café on Fisherman's Wharf. As we watched the sun set over the Golden Gate Bridge, I raised my first-ever glass of Irish coffee and proposed a toast to her memory.

"To Mrs. Reed!" I said.

"Who's Mrs. Reed?" one of my puzzled and slightly buzzed friends asked.

"A classy lady who taught me a whole lot about grace in the face of adversity."

27. The "Nearly Killed by Kindness" Blues

I WAS SIXTEEN and standing at the corner of Fifty-ninth Street and Lexington Avenue in midtown Manhattan. I was waiting for a friend who was planning on shopping at Bloomingdale's across the street. We often joked that someday she'd be late to her own funeral, and that day proved no different. It was about five in the afternoon and the sidewalks were crowded with people busily rushing to and from work and shopping for the holidays. I'd recently gotten my first iconic white-and-red cane, which I was holding at my side while I waited. My eyesight back then could best be described as looking at the world through glasses heavily smeared with Vaseline.

Without warning, a large hand grabbed my biceps and I suddenly found myself being frog-marched across Lexington Avenue. Judging by the screeching of tires, blaring of horns, and cursing cabbies, we were crossing against the light. Too stunned to resist, I looked up and could just make out a large man looming beside me. He was wearing a white hard hat, and his grip was so ironclad that there was no hope of wriggling free.

Over the din of the protesting traffic and construction site jackhammers, I looked up and asked, "What ya doing, mister?"

It must have been about then that the light turned green because we were quickly engulfed by a wave of people rushing across Lexington in the opposite direction. Like a football lineman opening a hole for his running back, he was totally preoccupied clearing the pedestrian crosswalk for us. Turning to me midstreet, he said,

"Thought you'd need a hand crossing Lex. It being crazy this time of day and you being blind and all."

The man had to be at least six foot five and probably topped the scales at three hundred pounds. I suppressed my urge to laugh out loud. Instead, I said, "Actually, I'm fine. I was kinda waiting for my friend back there."

Just then we reached the opposite corner, and he easily hoisted me up onto the sidewalk and released his viselike clasp on my arm. Shaking his massive head slowly, he finally got around to asking, "You didn't want to cross?"

"Not really, but thanks for the lift," I snarked.

He seemed mildly annoyed as he proceeded to walk away down Fifty-ninth Street. Ten steps down the block he turned and shouted, "You need me to take you back across?"

In theory, kindness, like grace, is one of the more important qualities a human can possess. But kindness can become a quality that can sometimes slip into pity. So when disability activists go about challenging stories about being on the receiving end of "kindness," some people become uncomfortable. In *Time* magazine the activist Rebekah Taussig wrote, "I've found people's attempts to Be Kind can be anything from healing to humiliating, helpful to traumatic. . . . The main messaging surrounding disabled people is that we're supposed to Be Nice to them (or maybe its close cousin, Don't Be Mean)."

While the treatment experienced by many people of color at the hands of some Whites can include fear, ignorance, suspicion, and hate, the treatment of the disabled at the hands of the nondisabled leans more toward kindness but just as often veers into a custodial form of pitying, infantilization, or paternalistic sympathy.

* * *

Three years after the episode on Lexington Avenue in Manhattan, I was in a pub in London, England, near closing time. It was 1974 and I was an international student studying therapeutic recreation. Unfortunately, my eyesight had recently deteriorated to the point that I was forced to use my cane at night. I'd been reluctant, as it made me feel vulnerable and I knew it carried a stigma. (Years later a gay friend would observe that hiding my cane in my backpack was like a form of being "in the closet" for some GLBT folks.) Lilly, one of my classmates, was aware of my condition and offered to walk with me back to the Underground stop. Lilly reminded me of Christie Brinkley, except she had shoulder-length chestnut-brown hair and was shorter and squatter. Being smitten, and more than a little drunk on English bitter, I happily agreed.

Not familiar with how to guide blind folks, Lilly held me by the back of my triceps and nudged me a half step ahead of her. At a distance, you might have assumed I was leading her. Unwisely, I put my folding cane in my back pocket. As we walked in the dark she and I fell into a deep conversation about the coal strike in England, and then about our respective boyfriend and girlfriend statuses.

Three sheets to the wind, Lilly turned to me and confessed, "I kind of have a boyfriend back in Cortland named John. We're on a break right now." Before I could react, suddenly I experienced a large crushing thud to my forehead. Lilly had walked me headfirst into a bobby's call box. At that time, London's iconic bobbies strategically positioned red metal call boxes on poles throughout the city in case of emergencies. Sprawled flat on my back, I felt like I was in a *Looney Tunes* cartoon as swirling stars exploded before my eyes—except it hurt like hell!

"Oh God, oh God," she cried. "I'm so sorry. Didn't you see the box?"

Four months later we were back in the United States, and despite our rocky start, I was still pursuing a long-shot relationship with Lilly. One fine September day, she drove me to the nearby campus of Cornell University in Ithaca, New York. We arrived just as the sun was setting, and the views of the waterfalls at Ithaca Gorge were spectacular. But the roar of the water careening off the cliff's edge made conversation difficult. We decided to walk along the rim of the gorge so we could hear ourselves talk. Even with my limited eyesight, the deepening red and yellow fall colors were stunning, highlighted by the orange of the setting sun. Sixty feet below, the sounds of the rushing river were softly gurgling up.

Typical of young lovers wrapped in one another's gaze, I was unaware of much else. The gorge is a large horseshoe-shaped canyon, and, since it's a primitive trail, there were no guardrails. As we came up to a turn on the path, the intensifying shadows played havoc with my lack of depth perception. Not sensing the approaching turn and looking only at Lilly, I continued to stroll ahead, and . . . straight off the cliff.

In midair, there was a moment when I thought *Oh Shit!* Then I landed hard on my butt and began to rapidly slide feet first down the steep precipice. I was vaguely aware that Lilly was screaming, but I was too busy desperately grasping for a hand or foothold to respond. Fifteen feet down the cliff I slid into a patch of immature cedar trees and grabbed onto a slender trunk to arrest my fall toward oblivion. Catching my breath, I turned onto my belly. Slowly I began the long, painful process of inching my way back up the cliff. Finally, I was able to roll belly first back onto the trail. I was scratched and bleeding, and my adrenaline had played out. Exhausted, I stayed lying on the ground, face up.

Hovering, Lilly kept asking "Are you hurt? Are you hurt?"

Later I'd learn that two or three deaths were recorded at the gorge every year. Perhaps anticipating a tragic death, or at least a dramatic rescue, a small group of college coeds gathered around us. A White male student wearing a Cornell sweatshirt leaned toward my face and, laughing, said, "Man, didn't you see the washout? What are ya, blind?" Too spent to come up with a snappier retort, I replied, "Fuck you, idiot. Yeah, I am blind."

That is when I learned to sing "The Nearly Killed by Blindness Blues." Lying there, it hit me that perhaps something had to be done about my intensifying blindness. Within a month, my mother would arrange for me to undergo an experimental eye procedure using ultrasonic waves. It could remove the diseased lens and cataract and replace it with an artificial lens that would theoretically restore the sight in my failing right eye. Or, potentially, leave me totally blind in both eyes.

People with disabilities comprise about 20 percent of the population and are America's largest minority group. A concise way of defining ableism is the disempowerment of people with disabilities at the interpersonal, cultural, and institutional levels. Ableism, like racism and other "isms," serves to normalize and privilege one group of people at the expense of others. Constructing buildings, restrooms, and phone apps that are only accessible to the able-bodied excludes those with certain disabilities. One classic example of cultural ableism is telethons like Jerry Lewis's for muscular dystrophy, which evoked pity by imagining the disabled as helpless and powerless children.

While ableism shares similarities with other forms of bias, there are several things that set ableism apart. One is the idea of Cure: that unless one's disability is removed (through a miracle of modern medicine, Charity, or Divine Intervention), a person with a disability will always be perceived as less than a fully capable human. I was soon to wrestle with this dilemma as I was about to face "corrective eye surgery."

A second unique dimension is that, unlike the case with racial bias, nearly all "temporarily" able-bodied people will someday become disabled themselves. During my teaching career, I found that people who might otherwise be resistant to exploring racial oppression were more open to looking at ableism, perhaps because they sensed their own vulnerability. It was also not uncommon for participants to have a relative with a disability—not always the case for White folks struggling with racism.

And finally, there's the dilemma I experienced firsthand, the double-edged sword of "kindness" or "pity." Once, opening a door for a woman, she called me out as she found my attempt at chivalry not as an act of "kindness," but as an implicit statement about her being less capable, or the "weaker sex." It wasn't until I connected how some able-bodied folks treat people with disabilities that I understood how my chivalry colluded with sexism. Being tracked into typing classes or away from college and toward a job selling newspapers at a kiosk were examples of systemic, institutional ableism. In *Time*, Jessica Smith explains institutional ableism succinctly: "Viewing disability through a social lens also means acknowledging that a person is more disabled by their environment and the discrimination of others than by their actual disability."

Rebekah Taussig reminds us that like all human beings, disabled people are both capable and, at times, may need some help. This can leave well-intentioned folks stuck in a quandary. What do they do or say around disabled people? "Remember to ask if [a person with a disability] wants help. If you want to genuinely, actively be 'kind' to disabled people . . . do your best to make the world accessible to them," Taussig suggests. I would add to practice seeing the person first, and the disability second. Not by coincidence, the same advice applies to race, gender, sexual orientation, religion, social class, etc. Please note that this is not the same as practicing "color blindness," the tendency to pretend racial difference doesn't exist.

Shortly after my trip to Ithaca Falls (get the pun?), Lilly and I stopped seeing one another. To cushion the blow to my ego, I told friends that luckily for my health, she had decided to give John another chance. In truth, I was laid low once again by my recurring fears of rejection, abandonment, and now, my diminishing eyesight.

28. Seeing in Technicolor

All this universe is in this eye of mine.
—SEPPO (ZEN BUDDHIST MASTER)

FORCED TO LEAVE LONDON in the fall of 1974, now lying on the operating table about to succumb to anesthesia, my parting words to Dr. Feldman were "Don't fuck this up." Wearing designer gold-rimmed glasses, he was an expensive Park Avenue eye surgeon about to perform innovative and potentially life-changing eye surgery on me. You might ask, "Why would you antagonize the man?" Because I was an anxious, annoyed working-class New York teenager and he was an arrogant, rich celebrity surgeon who gave clients only ten minutes of his precious time, if you were lucky. If not for my mother once again calling on her connections at the *Long Island Press,* I'd never have even gotten an appointment.

In his world I was just another procedure. Even to this day, few medical schools teach doctors about the lived experiences of their blind patients. During the intake appointment, when my ten minutes passed he had gotten up and walked to his mahogany office door to signal our appointment was over.

"I have a few more questions," I said.

"Sorry, but I'm very busy and other people are waiting," he said.

"Hey, this is my only good eye you're fucking with, so make the time. Besides, I don't see any bouncers in your lobby." Dressed in my black leather jacket and full Afro, I looked every bit the stereotype of a Puerto Rican thug.

After adjusting his glasses, he said, "Go on, ask your questions."

Now, eight weeks later, I was being wheeled into the operating room already under the influence of the anesthesia. I was groggy and the bright lights were increasingly blurry, but when he came over to do a pre-op check on me, I still managed to utter my warning.

He didn't fuck it up. When I woke up I was in a recovery room in New York's Manhattan Eye and Ear Hospital with both eyes covered with gauze. I couldn't see a thing, but I remember hearing my mother's anxious voice.

"Jimmy, the doctor said it went very well." I heard her sniffle and then blow her nose. She asked, "Do you feel any pain?" Before I could answer she added, "I couldn't sleep at all. I'm so relieved it's over."

Because I couldn't watch TV, the only distraction I had was a Slinky toy. The rhythmic sound of the Slinky as it flowed from my left hand to my right hand, back and forth, again and again, proved comforting.

Early the next morning the celebrity surgeon appeared to remove the bandages. Feldman explained, "We covered both eyes to limit extraneous movement." The first sight I saw was him rising up to his full five-foot-four height as he said, "The surgery was a complete success."

I should have been grateful, but the night before the surgery I'd been panicking about just those exact words. *What if I'm no longer a blind person? What if I suddenly become sighted? Who will I be then?* Having spent more than half of my nineteen years of life legally blind, I was terrified. I'd developed into a high-functioning young blind man, able to work as a counselor in a camp for the blind, capable of attending college and even studying in London. I thought of myself as the poster boy for the well-adjusted, successful, high-performing disabled person. I'd taken the hand Life had dealt me and assembled my identity accordingly. I liked the Legally Blind Me. Why would I want to be just another member of sighted society indistinguishable from the hordes?

Tossing and turning, switching the television on and off, I worked myself into such a lather that a night nurse came in and kindly offered me some sleeping meds. A large Black woman, she immediately put me at ease with her matter-of-fact demeanor.

"Sweetie, Feldman performs about forty of these a week and I ain't seen him botch one yet. And I've been here seven years. He can't afford to, what with his payments on his Manhattan penthouse, Bahamian beach house, and two Beamers. You'll be just fine, believe me," she said.

Although she misinterpreted my terror, I began to feel a little embarrassed about my emotional state. "I think I'll be fine now. Thanks," I said.

Sans medication, I eventually got myself to sleep, but later I dreamed of being trapped in a cage with no sides.

My mother, too nervous to drive, left her car in Queens and took a cab. Later that afternoon, after the bandages were removed, I was discharged and a hospital security guard hailed us a yellow-checkered cab. Solicitously, the cabby grabbed my arm and, "helping," literally dragged me into the backseat of the idling cab. I was thinking, *God, this guy must have painted his taxi psychedelic yellow so it would stand out—it's so intense!*

It was late afternoon and the cabbie's route took us through Central Park. It was early October and the red of the setting sun gave the changing leaves a fiery glow. Every single thing I saw—the painted horse-drawn carriages, the joggers' sweatpants, dogs walking with their masters—shimmered with glorious detail. I'd never imagined the orange of the oaks and scarlet of the maples could be so vivid. Even passing cars seemed to radiate all the hues of the color wheel. It was dizzy-making, akin to what I imagined tripping on LSD was like.

A bisexual friend once explained to me that her first husband had been sexually "okay." "Just fine," she said, "like a black-and-white film. But being with a woman was like seeing in Technicolor for the first time. There was just no going back." That's how I experienced seeing clearly for the first time in ten years. Before, I saw my world pass by in dull shades of black, white, and gray. As we drove past the natural beauty of New York City's premier urban park, Central Park's stately sycamores and birches glowed like embers in a campfire. The maple leaves were so brilliantly crimson that I could feel my blood vessels pulsating in response. From the backseat of that cab, I knew that I'd never see Nature in the same way again. I'd passed through a new threshold. I'd vacated my one-dimensional world of monochromatic color for one of multicolored immersion. My journey with physical sight had begun.

29. Learning to Drive

FOR A VISUALLY IMPAIRED TEENAGE BOY there was no greater imagined freedom than the freedom to drive. For nineteen years, I'd been at the mercy of others driving me places they wanted to go or arranged for me. Going to Lighthouse for the Blind's Saturday recreation program, I was picked up by their station wagon for the thirty-five-minute drive from Queens into Manhattan. Maureen O'Brien normally rode the Lighthouse station wagon in from Queens with me, but one spring Saturday four months after our sit-in victory, her customary seat was empty. "So where is our Miss O'Brien today?" I asked.

A big man, our driver Sean reached onto the dashboard and put on his dark aviator sunglasses. There was a long pause before he spoke. Choking back the slightest of sobs, in his lilting Irish brogue he said, "Maureen died from a heroin overdose last night. They found her in her room this morning when I came to pick her up." My chest suddenly tightened and I found it difficult to breathe.

Maureen was the lively gal who had become my first political mentor, introducing me to the world of sit-ins and protests. I had a girlfriend named Patty Wade, who was partially sighted, a fantastic dancer, and an equally talented make-out artist. But O'Brien had been my gal pal. She and I had shared confidences, laughs, sorrows, and teenage confusions. It was impossible to grasp that she was gone.

Like our Irish immigrant driver, Maureen was raised in a strict Catholic household. Months back, she'd confided in me how she was experimenting with marijuana, speed, LSD, and eventually "H" (horse, aka heroin). Like too many blind teenagers, depression was an ongoing demon Maureen, and later I, struggled with. I felt guilty that I'd never picked up on her unhappiness.

Sean and I were the only two people in the Crown Vic wagon that day, and the rest of the drive into Manhattan passed by in silence. It felt like an out-of-body experience. I realized Maureen's was the first death of anyone I'd cared for personally. It didn't feel real, and for months afterward I'd expect to see her on Saturdays as I'd climb into Sean's car.

Eventually, even though it took a long time, I stopped taking the station wagon to Lighthouse and instead took public transportation. The idea of Maureen's empty seat in the Crown Vic was too painful. It was during the long bus and subway trips to Lighthouse in Manhattan that an idea first took root. If I could drive I'd be freed from the onerous fifty-five-minute bus and train ride. "I can play whatever music meets my fancy," I rationalized. Maureen and I would childishly argue over what station to tune in on Sean's radio. She argued for folk: Judy Collins, Joan Baez, Bob Dylan. I'd argue for Motown: Otis Redding, the Supremes, Marvin Gaye.

Finally, Sean would have to step in, saying, "You two put me in mind of my cat and dog, always scrappin'. Enjoy this fine day and give me some peace, would ya?"

Some Saturday mornings, after a particularly hot argument with my mother, I simply wanted quiet in the car on the ride into Lighthouse, not possible with the ever-chatty Maureen. But now that she was gone, I sorely missed her and felt hollowed out inside.

I so desperately wanted to be able to drive myself that after Maureen's death my desire for independence crystalized. I got my wish four years later, after my cataract surgery. My mother was an awful driver; she was anxious, combative, and easily flummoxed, and she got lost regularly. Dee was the poster child for road rage. Thankfully, it was my stepfather John, a painfully quiet presence in the house, who spoke up and insisted she get me private driving lessons. I took to driving like a duck takes to water. Although I had only one good eye (I was still blind in my left eye even after the surgery), I was a natural. After my probationary period, John would loan me his red, wood-paneled 1974 Caprice station wagon. It drove like a boat, but I couldn't care less.

Within hours of my visits home from college, Dee and I would inevitably get on each other's nerves. But now that I had a license, I had an escape hatch! "John, can I practice driving with the wagon?" I'd ask. Sensing an explosion about to erupt between mother and son, John was only too glad to oblige. So on a Friday evening, off I cruised into New York City, down Atlantic Avenue through Brooklyn toward the Brooklyn Bridge and into lower Manhattan. Along the way I'd drive through Atlantic Avenue's rich cultural tapestry of African American, Puerto Rican, Italian, and Irish neighborhoods.

At first glance, driving at night would seem harder for a novice driver, especially one with newly minted eyesight. But I found the darkness liberating. Nightfall in the city filtered out needless distractions, not unlike TV's *CSI* sleuths inspecting crime scenes in the dark with flashlights. Crossing the Brooklyn Bridge, I'd zip along at seventy miles an hour down FDR Drive, passing slower cars like Mario Andretti. The twinkling lights of the Manhattan skyline were my dazzling companions.

When I tired of the quiet and being alone, I'd tune in WBAI radio to groove to its Motown and jazz sounds as I tooled around Manhattan. I'd stay out for hours, timing my return to be sure Dee was fast asleep. My implicit contract with John was that I'd always leave his gas tank full. It was a price I was all too happy to pay for a night of automotive adventure and family peace. On some nights, I yearned to hear Maureen's happy voice next to me.

30. "Crip Camp"

LIKE SO MANY GREAT ROMANCES, my newfound love of being able to drive hit a bad patch two years after my eye surgery. I was working at Jened, a camp for people with disabilities, as the Waterfront Director. One day the camp director handed me the keys to the official camp station wagon and had me run errands in Hunter, New York.

I was unfamiliar with the vehicle. As I was attempting to back out of a busy gas station, thinking I was in reverse, I mistakenly hit the gas pedal while still in first gear. I proceeded to ram into the massive steel bumper of a huge, bright yellow and green Hess gasoline tanker. The driver, a tall, lanky Sam Shepard lookalike, slowly stepped down from the truck's cab. Shaking, I met him halfway to worriedly inspect damage to the truck. Not only was his bumper undented, but miraculously there wasn't even a scratch to his paint job.

Adjusting the brim of his trucker's hat and shaking his head, he drawled, "Well, I guess I'm okay." Turning toward the wagon, he smiled and said, "Looks like you might of got the worst of it. Tell you what, let's skip all the damn paperwork and call it a day. Do we have a deal?"

I sighed a long breath of relief. As a twenty-one-year-old with a brand-new driver's license, I figured I'd just dodged a bullet. With that, he pulled his long frame up into the tanker's cab and drove away, waving out the window.

Then, I turned and looked more closely at the camp wagon.

The hood was so crumpled it resembled an accordion. Fortunately, it drove well enough and returned me to camp without further incident. But the shame of my first accident was too much to bear. Shortly after explaining to the camp director what happened, I took to my private cabin, where I hid for the next three days feigning a cold. Not until the camp wagon's hood had been replaced did I dare show my face.

How I stumbled into my job at Camp Jened was thanks to none other than Roger, the former director at Camp Lighthouse. Roger had been hired as Jened's new director and, on hearing of my successful eye operation and subsequent lifeguard certification, offered me the Waterfront Director's job. Having broken his nose at Lighthouse, I no longer feared Roger. And so, being a newly minted water safety instructor who loved summer camps, I quickly accepted.

That's how, on a lovely spring day, I drove with Roger and the assistant camp director, Lee, onto the grounds of Willowbrook State School on Staten Island for a screening of potential new Camp Jened campers. From the outside, it resembled an old college campus, brick buildings with gray-green roofs sprawled out over eighty acres. But inside, the reality was nothing like college life.

A year earlier, Willowbrook had made national headlines when a young reporter by the name of Geraldo Rivera snuck a camera into the facility. He revealed residents in filthy clothes or sitting naked on cold tile floors for lack of a clean change. Rivera's report documented residents in a constant state of neglect, including serious physical and sexual abuse. One Harvard student wrote about his summer job at Willowbrook, where he routinely witnessed forty-five adolescents huddled in a room, given no structure, "moaning and screaming, rocking back and forth, stinking of urine and feces." But even following a class-action lawsuit, conditions had not changed markedly by the time we visited a year later.

It was still a foul and smelly institution that remained chronically understaffed. As we walked the units, the stench and occasional shrieks were unnerving. Although it was well past lunch, we came upon clients unable to dress themselves who were left in soiled pajamas. After just two hours in that oppressive setting I yearned to go outside into the sunshine and smell the cool spring breeze. Little wonder that residents we interviewed begged us to bring them to camp. The appeal of mountain air, outdoor recreation, and an escape from Willowbrook was totally understandable. One camper named Nancy cried during our screening interview at just the idea of escaping to a camp in the Catskill Mountains. Two months later Nancy would be out of her wheelchair, sporting sunglasses as she floated blissfully in Jened's heated pool while I held her head above water. Thanks to the warm water, through my arms I could feel the easing of the chronic muscle tightness caused by her cerebral palsy. It is a memory that remains permanently etched in my mind.

"It was so funky!" said a former Jened camper, Denise Jacobson, in a documentary on Jened. "But it was Utopia when we were there, there was no outside world."

Having been a camper at Camp Lighthouse only four years earlier, I understood that finding young love was one of the many normal joys of summer camp, And one of my dearest recollections from Jened is of two campers in love. Eric was nineteen and missing both arms from an electric utility accident. His camp sweetheart Ange was eighteen and because of severe cerebral palsy, which caused uncontrolled spasms and occasional seizures, used a wheelchair. One night Ange and Eric convinced their respective female and male counselors to show them how they might have intercourse despite their physical limitations. Remember this was the 1970s and the era of free love. Relying on their counselors as coaches and assistants, Ange and Eric learned how to consummate their relationship just like many "normal" teenagers of the time.

Jened also had a legendary camper who came from Willowbrook named Scott. Moderately developmentally disabled, Scott had been coming to Jened for years. But he had a "special medical problem" that only Camp Jened seemed able to cure. Scott was unable to move his bowels at Willowbrook for an entire year. The Willowbrook staff would try everything to help him have a bowel movement, but nothing worked. The only remedy that had proven effective over the years was when Scott came to Jened and fully relaxed. Year after year the same ritual would enfold. Senior Jened counselors familiar with Scott's condition would line his cabin's toilet with black ten-gallon garbage bags to "safeguard the camp's septic system." After about three days at camp Scott would then proceed to unload himself for the better part of an afternoon. I watched in stunned disbelief as his counselors made repeated trips down the rickety ramp hauling away a year's worth of Scott's excrement to the dumpster in black Hefty bags. Although Scott's relief of being out of Willowbrook was extreme, like Nancy, his joy at being at Jened was palpable (and measurable as well).

Eventually, the horrors of Willowbrook would spur a national outcry and lead to the deinstitutionalization movement, whose aim was to get people with disabilities out of institutions like Willowbrook and into community settings and small group homes. But for change to happen it would take the idealism of a new generation of younger Americans. People I know think of hippies as a phenomenon of the past, but gains for people of color, gay and lesbian Americans, and those with disabilities would've been impossible without this generation. However, the story of progress for people with disabilities and the important role of Camp Jened remained unknown to millions of Americans, including me.

That changed in 2020 with the release of *Crip Camp: A Disability Revolution*. The film documented how a group of young activists with disabilities pressed for the signing of the Americans with Disabilities Act (ADA) of 1990. But their movement had taken root decades earlier, with the civil rights movement, and then with the push for deinstitutionalization, and at a summer camp called Jened. Camp Jened was in operation from 1950 to 1977. As former camp codirector James LeBrecht, himself a Jened attendee, put it in the film, "This camp kind of changed the world, and nobody knows the story."

I worked at Camp Jened in the summer of 1976, the year before it closed due to its deteriorating condition. It sat in the middle of a floodplain, and the risky prospect of having to quickly evacuate a camp full of people in wheelchairs hastened its demise. The film combined archival and news footage with present-day interviews to draw a direct line from Camp Jened to the passage of the ADA. Many who attended Jened in the 1970s expressed that it was the first time they felt seen, heard, and acknowledged as individuals.

Before seeing the documentary I'd considered Jened just another summer camp, unaware that it was a funnel that fed young leaders into the disability rights movement.

Much of *Crip Camp* focused on Judy Heumann, a Jened counselor who went on to become a pivotal leader in the disability civil rights movement. In 1973 Heumann spearheaded a twenty-four-day sit-in at the San Francisco office of the Department of Health, Education, and Welfare. That sit-in helped get a federal civil rights statute signed into law that banned discrimination based on disability. But the victory wasn't enough for Judy and the blossoming disability rights movement. During a meeting with fellow activists, she expressed her ongoing frustration: "I'm tired of being thankful for accessible toilets."

Judy's rebelliousness symbolized the fight to not just say "No thank you!" to ableism but also say "Yes!" to equity. It helped ignite a spirit of social justice that took many former Jened campers to California, where eventually they would change the world. At the close of Camp Jened that summer, influenced by what I'd seen and experienced, I moved to California myself and soon joined that struggle.

31. Stumbling into Spirit in Nature

> Wherever you are, you are one with the clouds and one
> with the sun and the stars you see. You are one with everything.
> That is more true than I can say, and more true than you can hear.
> —SHUNRYŪ SUZUKI

THROUGH MY EXPERIENCES at Camp Lighthouse and in college, I was beginning to see that Mother Earth would, at critical moments, beckon to me spiritually. It was 1976, and I was standing directly under the biggest tree I'd ever seen in my life. To no one, I said, "No way there are trees like this back in Queens!" I was beholding my first Pacific Coast Redwood. Alone, I felt no self-consciousness as I embraced the Old Giant. My outstretched arms barely embraced a tenth of the girth of the colossal trunk. Its canopy climbed so high I couldn't see the crown or the sky above. Its energy filled me with the realization of how small we humans really are, and a humble sense of my place in God's universe.

That summer I was working as a college intern at a camp in the Santa Cruz Mountains of California and it was my day off. That morning I'd gotten a letter from a girlfriend of two years announcing she'd met someone else back in New York. As a balm for my pain, I decided I needed some time in the woods alone.

Saying goodbye to the Old Giant, I followed a steep trail as it led up the mountain to a clearing with a lone tepee fashioned by the camp's nature counselor. It was late afternoon and the site was deserted, so I bent down and made my way within. Inside it smelled of pine boughs, damp earth, and mildew. Except for a long, narrow shaft of light emanating from the smoke hole at the tepee's apex, the space was dark and cool. I settled down and began a meditation I'd recently learned while reading Carlos Castaneda's *Teachings of Don Juan*. Sitting cross-legged, looking up through the smoke hole, I took in deep breaths to open myself to the beauty of the moment. The only sounds were the wind blowing through the redwoods and the occasional chatter of a chipmunk. After my mediation I became drowsy and lay down on a blanket, tired from the hike. I fashioned an old blanket into a pillow and was soon fast asleep.

I awoke to complete darkness, unaware of how much time had passed. As I swam up from a reverie, the call of an owl echoed through the shreds of my fading dream. Fully awake, I quietly crawled out through the tepee's flap on my hands and knees into the surrounding darkness. As I climbed to my feet, the nearby call of a real owl caused me to freeze. Cautiously, I fumbled for the switch on my flashlight and pointed the beam up into the forest's darkened canopy. The evening had grown cool and there were fingers of fog floating in the air. What I caught in the beam's glow was a huge Great Horned Owl in a nearby tree. It swiveled its head in my direction and stared down at me. The yellow glow of its massive eyes was illuminated by the flashlight's beam. It blinked once. Unsure of my next move, I simply said, "Sorry to disturb you, Brother Owl." As if in response, it hooted three times, then lifted and stretched its vast wings and flew off soundlessly into the shadows. I recalled then that Don Juan described owls as messengers of mourning from the Spirit World announcing Death. Was it acknowledging my dead romance?

Whether due to my close encounter with the owl, my meditation, or my nap, all my senses were now on full alert. Since the steep trail back to camp was enveloped in a wet misty blackness, I was forced to make my way down it carefully. I was about a quarter mile from the camp when I became aware of the sound of crackling twigs to my left. Having been forewarned about the presence of black bears in the area, a sense of dread crept down my back. I resisted the urge to aim my flashlight toward the sounds and proceeded another fifty yards. But once more the nearby rustling betrayed the fact that I was not alone. Unable to control my fear, I swung the flashlight's beam in the direction of my uninvited nighttime companion. Two fiery white eyes stared back at me through the gloom. I judged that it was too short to be a bear, but too tall to be a fox or a skunk.

Emboldened by the thought that it wasn't a bear, I decided to step off the trail to get a closer look. I quickly realized I'd made a big mistake. My change of direction elicited a deep, guttural growling that stopped me in my tracks. Thinking better of indulging my curiosity, I slowly reversed my steps. Struggling to contain the urge to run, I continued back down the path towards the camp. As I moved down the trail, I occasionally swung the beam to my left. The glowing white eyes were keeping pace, but no further growling occurred. When I was about thirty yards from our cabin, the white eyes vanished as quietly as they had first appeared. I was overtaken by a sense of relief—but also a sense of loss.

The next morning, puzzled by my strange encounter, I sought out the camp's naturalist to share the excitement of my two sightings. She was enthusiastic about the story of the Great Horned Owl but became quiet when I told her of being followed by "fiery white eyes." We retraced my steps to the spot where I had first heard sounds off the trail. She stooped down and examined some droppings. "That's coyote scat," she said definitively. "And it's very fresh. They're smaller than a wolf but have been known to take down animals as large as deer or young elk when they hunt in packs."

A puff of breath escaped my lungs. I'd never seen a coyote in the wild. In *The Teachings of Don Juan*, coyotes figure prominently as tricksters. "Phew, that was amazing, and so close!" I muttered. As the words left my mouth, I felt excitement and relief simultaneously, not unlike the sensation of flying through the air on a rope swing while hoping it doesn't snap.

"Kinda weird," the naturalist said. "Coyotes usually shy away from humans up here, unless . . . they're rabid."

Her words should have perhaps given me pause. But all I sensed in that moment was a deep gratitude for my close encounter with the Nature Spirits of the Santa Cruz Mountains. Like the swim dock experience back at Camp Lighthouse or the Old Oak in Cortland, I realized this wasn't the first time Mother Earth had consoled my wounded Spirit. Robin Wall Kimmerer's words in *Braiding Sweet-*

grass, "Alone is a word without meaning in the forest," were coming to make perfect sense to me.

I spent a total of two and a half years in California working at the Pomeroy Center for children and adults with disabilities. After my initial internship in 1975, I was hired back a year later, which is how I came to work at the camp in the Santa Cruz Mountains. Even though I loved San Francisco, back at Camp Jened I'd fallen for a New York gal and ended up returning to the East Coast in late 1977 to be with her. But before I could return, she had taken up with a new guy. Unfortunately, it was not the last time I'd be left out in the cold by her.

Luckily, friends from London told me of an amazing outdoor education community in Dover Plains, New York. Having already resigned my San Francisco job, I took a position at Dover Environmental Education Center (DEEC) as an apprentice naturalist. DEEC was a program affiliated with the New York City Mission Society. Nestled within 1,400 acres of wooded forest and ponds, DEEC had three dormitories for kids who came up from the city and the suburbs to participate in its outdoor education programs. But that's where the similarities with other, more traditional outdoor programs ended.

DEEC was an intentional community of seventeen naturalists who governed it using an anarchist model of consensus drawn from the book *Resource Manual for a Living Revolution.* Preferring to be called "members," not staff, we shared communal living and eating arrangements in a twelve-room main building on site. Our dining hall was run by a former chef from Albany, and the menu was completely vegetarian—and delicious! Each week at the community meeting, we'd review how the coming week would unfold, assign duties, and solve any issues that might have arisen. In the spirit of equity, facilitation for these meetings rotated among all the members equally. It was as close as I would ever come to the legendary hippie communes of the 1960s. We ate well, worked hard, and reveled in our proximity and relationship to the natural world. Even though I was the only person of color, I wondered, *Have I finally found a family?*

My most prized recollection of Dover is when three busloads

of students arrived with kids from Harlem. Most had never been off the island of Manhattan, and the wilds of Dover were new and frightening to many. On the final night, so that the kids might have a sensory experience unlike any they'd had in the noise and bright lights of the city, we organized a night hike into DEEC's oak forest.

As we broke into small groups, I was given charge of four Black preteen girls. As I was leading them by flashlight into the darkened woods, they soon froze in place, refused to go any farther, and promptly sat down. Going with the group's flow, I sat down with them in their circle. I began by sharing that I was also a New York City kid.

"What scares you about the woods?" I asked gently.

Gathered around the glow of my upturned flashlight, they took turns calling out their fears.

"Shee-at, I can't see my hand in front of my fucking face," said one.

"I'm afraid of all these weird noises coming from over there," said another, pointing into the woods.

"There's probably a maniac waiting in there for us!" volunteered another.

After ten minutes of letting them express their fears, I said, "What if I told you all these White naturalists wouldn't step one foot in Harlem because they're afraid of what they don't know?" In the soft glow of the flashlight, I could see one of the youngest, wearing pigtails, mulling over my question. "What are you thinking, Charlotte?" I asked.

Sitting up straight, she looked around and then said, "What are they afraid of?"

"I guess they just don't know the neighborhood like you do."

"Hell," ventured one of the older girls, "there ain't nothing to be 'fraid of, especially if you know who's who. I think they just chicken 'cause they all White and afraid of us Black folk!"

"So," I said. "Sounds like you're saying people get afraid of things and places they don't know?"

In the dim light of the flashlight, I could make out heads bobbing up and down in agreement. At that moment a Barred Owl began hooting from deep inside the forest. Eyes wide, the girls huddled together and closer to me.

"That there's Mrs. Barred Owl." I offered. She's only about this big." I approximated two feet tall with my hands. "She comes out at night to hunt for mice for her babies. I don't think she'd confuse you for a little mouse, do you?"

"We have rats in my neighborhood big as cats," offered one. "I ain't afraid of them neither. Would Mrs. Owl eat a rat?"

"Hmm, I'm guessing a rat that size might scare Mrs. Owl senseless!"

Breaking the tension, the girls began to giggle, then eventually broke into peals of laughter. We sat in our circle for the remainder of the hour, never venturing further into the woods, instead discussing what came out of the woods after sunset. Several times the Barred Owl interrupted with her signature call, *Whooo cooks for you—whoooo cooks for you.*

"Why they do that?" asked Charlotte.

"Sometimes it's to warn other owls: 'Hey, this is my turf, so stay out.'" The girls seemed to understand this, and once again, heads nodded.

Asked another, "How comes they only come out at night?"

"During the day they'd have to fight with bigger birds like hawks, but at night they're the rulers of these woods. They have kind of a superpower that lets them hear and see in the dark."

We began imitating the owl by cupping our hands over our ears to simulate how they could find things in the dark by turning their heads side to side. Cupping her ears, one of the girls reported hearing the croaking of bullfrogs in a nearby pond, while another could suddenly make out crickets she hadn't noticed before. Little by little, my charges focused less on their fears and more on paying attention to the forest's symphony of sound. When I called back to the owl, it answered. The ripple of excitement in the circle was palpable.

By the time it was near for us to return to the indoor meeting room, Charlotte said, "I can see a whole lot better than before. I think you could turn off your flashlight now."

There was a murmur of protest from the other girls, but eventually I extinguished the light. Immediately, looking up, the group began spotting stars and, twice, a streaking meteor.

"We can't see those in the city," I said. "What if we go back now and let Charlotte guide us without the flashlight?"

We'd not stepped foot into the old oak forest, yet for me, the sight of four city girls, hands on each other's shoulders, being led by the diminutive and intrepid Charlotte, was my most memorable success as a naturalist.

32.   "With Correction"

SINCE MY SURGERY FIFTY YEARS AGO, I'm no longer legally blind. Although I still don't see from my left eye, with the help of a hard contact lens, the vision in my right eye has been restored to about 20/25. I sometimes refer to myself as a one-eyed stargazer. To be on the safe side, given the one eye, I have an eye exam annually. On one of my annual visits to an optometrist some years back, he used the term "with correction" in referring to my vision.

Driving back home after my appointment, my mind started to turn over the doctor's choice of words. In the nearly ten years I was legally blind, I rarely considered myself "in need of correction." Before my near breakdown the night of my eye surgery at nineteen, I rarely considered myself handicapped. True, in some circumstances I needed some help, but who doesn't? I didn't think of myself as "normal," but rarely did I see myself as less than. The exception was when my sight suddenly deteriorated in England.

The more I mulled over the implications of the phrase "with correction," the more other terms came flooding into me: Defective, Incorrect, Unwanted, Mistake, Unworthy, Less Than. Conversely, "without correction" could be interpreted as Normal, Desirable, Right, Average, Acceptable, Higher Functioning, Unlimited.

In this way of looking at the world, "needing correction" made me an outlier, the Other, undesirable, less confident, limited, requiring a fix, a deviant, or just plain wrong. A person like me in need of "correction" supposedly has a condition that requires neutralization or, maybe, elimination. It implies a mythical society populated by nondisabled people who are "correct" and, therefore, more desirable, trustworthy, and dependable.

It's not a huge leap to infer that the goal of a "corrected" society is one with no deviants, no defectives, no abnormal or disabled people. In other words, no unwanted conditions. History has shown that before Hitler put millions of Jews to death in his gas chambers, he first perfected his killing machines on tens of thousands of people with disabilities. Therefore, people like me should aspire to be correct or, at the very least, with correction, be seen as normal.

People whose eyesight is not correctable are often still labeled "handicapped," a term some believe has its origins in the Middle Ages. It references beggars with caps in hand begging for alms. "Handicapped" people have historically been seen as a drain on society, public charges, and an undesirable weight on public resources. President Trump once decreed that immigrants would be a drain on public resources and thus not welcome. That clearly implied that disabled or blind Latinos, like me, were especially unwelcome.

There are over one million Americans (about 1 in 320) who are legally blind, meaning that their "corrected" vision is less than 20/200. Most of my Lighthouse friends were low income. What I didn't know then is that we face poverty at twice the rate of our nondisabled peers. Since only 30 percent of disabled people of working age are employed, that legitimated my fear about getting and keeping a meaningful career. It's little wonder, as Andrew Leland notes in *The Country of the Blind*, "Blindness has reliably appeared at or near the top of the list of 'most feared disabilities' in polls and surveys for decades."

Like you, I'm sure, I'd heard of a few famous blind people—musical geniuses like Stevie Wonder, Andrea Bocelli, and Ray Charles, and of course the legendary author and activist Helen Keller. What I didn't learn from the 1962 five-time Academy Award–nominated movie *The Miracle Worker* was that Helen Keller was a suffragist, a radical political activist, and cofounder of the American Civil Liberties Union.

My doctor's choice of words got me wondering about other famous people with visual impairments I'd never heard of. Some of the names I found were surprising because I'd not associated them with being visually impaired. Consider this very partial list of individuals that were, or are, legally blind:

Harriet Tubman—American abolitionist and social activist who rescued approximately seventy enslaved people via the Underground Railroad.

James Thurber—American humorist, journalist, and playwright best known for his cartoons and short stories, published mainly in *The New Yorker* and in his books.

John Milton—English poet and intellectual whose epic poem *Paradise Lost* was written in 1667 during a time of immense religious and political upheaval.

Claude Monet—French painter and founder of the Impressionist School, a precursor to Modernism, famous for his paintings of Nature as he perceived it.

Horatio Nelson—His decisive British naval victories made him one of history's greatest naval commanders.

Franklin Delano Roosevelt—In addition to polio, our thirty-second president suffered from visual impairments as a result of his illness.

Wilma Mankiller—Activist and the first woman elected Principal Chief of the Cherokee Nation.

Jake Gyllenhaal—Oscar-nominated actor and winner of the BAFTA Award for the film *Brokeback Mountain*.

Jorge Luis Borges—Internationally renowned Argentine short-story writer, essayist, and poet.

Borges went blind at age fifty-five, never learned braille, and published forty books after he went blind. Andrew Leland quotes

Borges as saying, "Blindness for me has not been a total misfortune. It should not be seen in a pathetic way. It should be seen as a way of life, one of the styles of living."

So I found myself wondering, *What about the people on this list needed "correcting"?* Maybe those of us with correction should feel sorry for those of you who weren't corrected. Imagine what you might have accomplished.

33. All Roads Led to Community Organizing

Few will have the greatness to bend history itself, but each
of us can work to change a small portion of events and in the total
of all those acts will be written the history of this generation.
Each time a [wo]man stands up for an ideal, or acts to improve the
lots of others or strikes out against an injustice [s]he sends forth
a tiny ripple of hope, and . . . those ripples build a current that can
sweep down the mightiest walls of oppression and injustice.
—ROBERT F. KENNEDY

MY FAMILY'S HISTORY is riddled with political engagement, activism, and even violence. My great-grandfather Don Paco, on my father's side, was the target of an attempted assassination circa 1904 in Puerto Rico because of his politics. Riding a tall white mare through the center of the town of Mayagüez, Don Paco was charged at by a gunman wielding a large-caliber pistol. Don Paco's horse reared in fright, which caused the assassin to backpedal, forcing his shots to go wide. While the gunman was attempting to reload, the horse, with Don Paco hanging on for dear life, galloped away to safety.

Recall that my father's godfather was Pedro Albizu Campos, the Puerto Rican Independista of the 1940s and 1950s. Because of their affiliation with both Albizu Campos and the Independista movement, the family fled Puerto Rico under the threat of death. At the same time on the other end of the island's political divide, one of my mother's relatives was a National Guard colonel. He was killed when Independistas attempted to assassinate the U.S.-appointed Governor Blanton Winship.

Perhaps as a direct result of their families' divided political passions, my mother and my father were averse to politics. When it came to voting, my mother was fond of declaring, "They're all crooks, so why bother?"

My own introduction to politics began at fifteen at the sit-in at the offices of Lighthouse in Manhattan. My second experience came nine years later in California in the takeover of Governor Jerry Brown's offices. My next foray into the world of activism came at twenty-six when I was hired as the community organizer for a local Economic Opportunity Center (EOC) in Saratoga Springs, New York.

My first campaign at EOC was to help expose a county welfare commissioner named Joe Gemetti, who routinely denied benefits to needy and legally eligible applicants in the name of "fiscal conservatism." When he refused funds for an electric wheelchair, one that would have allowed a very disabled child to be semi-independent, he'd gone too far. EOC held a joint press conference with the family and the child. As a result of the ensuing firestorm of negative publicity for Saratoga County, the child not only got his wheelchair, but Gemetti was forced to retire within the year.

In my third year at EOC the director, Mack, summoned me into his office and said, "Close the door." Mack had proven a generous mentor, sending me to various workshops and trainings. I'd spent the last several months organizing a community fuel buyers' group (FBG). Participating members, many of whom were low income, saved hundreds of dollars on their home heating bills. FBG had been an unexpected success, and the income potential for EOC was surprisingly large. From the outset, Mack had given me his blessing to spin the FBG off from EOC. I'd recruited a high-powered local board of directors, and we were in the midst of attaining our own nonprofit status. I was on track to become one of the youngest agency nonprofit heads in upstate New York.

As I closed the door behind me, I anticipated a cordial separation and maybe a clap on the back. In my time with EOC, I'd led or co-led successful campaigns seeking county relief for low-income households, directed the home energy assistance program, founded a local food coop, and coordinated the citywide community gardens. But as I turned around to face Mack, I sensed today's was not to be a "Job well done, Jim!" meeting. He came from behind his desk and motioned me to sit at his small conference table. His manner was all business, with none of the political bantering and jokes that typified most of our meetings.

"I'm going to need the FGB board disbanded. FBG will become a satellite program of the EOC," he said. My wind temporarily knocked out of me, I paused to gather my thoughts before responding.

"But I've already assembled a board of directors. Wasn't that our agreement—that FBG would be its own independent organiza tion?"

When angered, Mack's nostrils flared, and his nostrils were now beginning to expand. "Yeah, well, the fucking Reagan administration just slashed the national EOC budget by 45 percent. We're going to need that income just to keep our doors open."

Now it was my turn to be pissed. "Are you going to tell the members of the FGB board?" I asked. It came across more as a dare, not as a question. For moment he and I locked eyes. Outside, I heard the sound of a garbage truck dumping a weekend's load of trash into its waiting maw.

He snarled, "It's your job to inform them, not mine. I expect you to draft a letter notifying them of this change. Have it on my desk for my approval first thing tomorrow morning."

Over the years, Mack had alienated a number of community leaders due to his sometimes brash, nonconsultative manner and infamous hot temper. With little forethought I said, "No, sir. I put my reputation on the line recruiting these people. Some of them would never have bought into an EOC-run project. I assured them from the outset that this would be an independent organization from EOC. I'm not going back on my word. I respect these people and myself too much."

He leaned forward so that his face was only three feet from mine. A wisp of his patchouli cologne wafted across my face. "Are you telling me you intend to disobey a direct order? That would be insubordination and grounds for immediate termination."

This was no empty threat. The year before I'd come to work at

EOC, Mack fired a slew of employees all in one day in an event that came to be known locally as the Friday Afternoon Massacre. I became aware that Mack's volume was carrying beyond his closed door and echoing throughout EOC's now silent offices.

Unwilling to back down, especially since I was being yelled at, in an equally loud voice I said, "Dude, do what you got to do."

Momentarily surprised, he sat back in his canvas director's chair. Quickly recovering, he said, "Be back in this office tomorrow morning at ten to meet with the Executive Personnel Committee. In the meantime, you're forbidden from discussing this with anyone inside or outside this agency."

I'd proven skillful at using the local press to shine a light on county or state misdeeds. and Mack was worried I might do the same to him. Shaking, I stood and went to my desk to gather my things. As I passed my coworkers' cubicles, they stared open-mouthed. Patti, our food stamp advocate, followed me out the door and caught up with me on the sidewalk outside.

"Jeez, Jim, what just happened in there? Everyone could hear Mack yelling."

Smiling weakly, I said, "I think I just got fired, but I'll know more tomorrow. I'm not 'allowed'"—I used air quotes for emphasis—"to discuss it."

Patti's face paled, and wordlessly she threw her arms around me. I welcomed the hug. Tears welled up in my eyes, but I turned and walked away to hide my embarrassment.

Unable to get either Mack or me to compromise, the next day the Personnel Committee hammered out a twenty-two-week severance package. Even with unemployment money, I quickly recognized I could no longer afford my cherished one-bedroom apartment. It was my first solo apartment ever, and I'd furnished and decorated it all on my own. The weight of being terminated and the imminent threat of homelessness settled in my chest, causing shortness of breath. Unbidden, memories of my driving-range fiasco and Dee throwing me out of my home when I took the Camp Lighthouse job came crashing in on me.

After the Personnel Committee meeting I was officially terminated. At ten in the morning I was unemployed. Walking home from EOC, I passed through the city of Saratoga Springs' lilac garden. Their sweet scent momentarily disarmed me. As Mother Earth was wont to do throughout my Life, Her gift to my senses forced me to step outside my immediate pain. The small act of opening myself to Her served as a temporary but necessary balm, akin to an embrace. In the garden's relative solitude, the tears finally flowed. The next six months would be among the most painful, yet the most expansive, of my twenty-six years.

34.   Dad and Son Reconcile

MEMORIES CAN BE HAPPY OR SAD. They are not the definitive truth. My earliest memory of my father is him slapping me for sitting too close to the television. I was five, and my congenital cataracts had yet to be diagnosed. In fairness, Dad had repeatedly cautioned me about sitting too near our new fourteen-inch black-and-white RCA television. But after obediently sliding back three feet from the screen, I'd unconsciously scooted closer to see the puppets' faces on *The Soupy Sales Show*.

The whack to the side of my head stunned me because I had no memory of my father hitting me before. The tears that followed were not from pain, but from wounded feelings. Before I could articulate that I was having trouble seeing the screen, my father walked out the apartment door for good. Unbeknown to me, that evening he and my mother had finally split up after years of bickering.

In the weeks and years that followed, afraid I'd done something to cause him to leave, I kept asking my mother what happened. "He's living with your grandmother now," she replied. "He watches TV all day and has no job. Who needs him! We're better off without him. He's a bum."

I knew I didn't feel better off without him. And of course, my young mind imagined it was my fault. *If only I hadn't sat so close to the TV.*

*   *   *

Thanks to my grandmother's iron will and insistent nature, my dad initially continued to come fetch me every other weekend for a visit. Our relationship was typified by his taking me to the Top Hat Bar, where he coached its adult baseball team. Once at Nana's, we'd sometimes play checkers, or I'd read *Boys' Life* magazine while he napped. As a treat, he and I would go out to his favorite Italian restaurant for dinner.

For years, my dad dated a pretty blonde Top Hat bartender named Mary. She was kind to me, giving me cherries for my "Coke on the rocks" and slipping me quarters to play the air-hockey table. I loved the heft and whooshing sound of the shiny metal puck when it slammed into the goal pocket. I also harbored a secret crush on Mary. After not visiting the Top Hat or hearing her name mentioned for several visits, I asked after her.

"She wanted to get married. I told her I'd been married before. When I told her that I wasn't getting married again, she cried. I wasn't willing to go through that hell again, so we split up," he said, lighting a Camel cigarette. I was sad over the news. I'd imagined that Mary would have made me a nice stepmommy.

By the time I was fifteen, Dad's visits became less frequent until almost a year passed without my seeing him. When he finally came to pick me up for our annual Christmas dinner with Nana, I was stunned. His dark black wavy hair had turned completely white. His snow-colored mane seemed to have mellowed him, so one weekend I worked up the courage to pose the question that haunted me ever since he'd left ten years earlier.

As we drove across the George Washington Bridge toward his and Nana's apartment in Fort Lee, New Jersey, I sat in the passenger seat of his black Cadillac. Screwing up my courage, I asked, "Viejo, how come you left me alone with Dee? Was it something I'd done? Something I'd said?"

He seemed genuinely surprised by the question. "Nah," he said. "It had nothing to do with you! She was an unreasonable woman, so emotional and out of control at times. She convinced all our friends at the *Long Island Press*, where we both worked back then, to hate me."

"Yeah, but you abandoned me as well."

Looking straight ahead as he steered into the sun, his reaction was not what I'd expected. In a flat tone he said, "It just wasn't working, we fought constantly." He quickly segued into a discussion of the Yankees and the upcoming baseball season, a favorite topic for him. I never posed the question again.

When I was twenty-one and living in San Francisco, I received a rare letter from him. Ever since the separation and divorce from my mother, my father had continued to live with his mother, Nana. I opened it one morning as I rode the outdated, green #33 streetcar to work. Reading the handwritten words on the yellow legal-sized page, I struggled to believe my one good eye:

November 15, 1976

Dear Jim:

The only way I can start this letter is by first saying that back in April I married a girl named Lucy: and I'm sure that when I tell you that I used to walk her by the hand when she was three (3) years old I know you won't believe me. I was eight and we were neighbors back in Puerto Rico. All I can tell you about her is that she has a heart as big as her. When you meet her you are going to be taken by her, as is everyone else.

Let me know how you're doing and how are you are liking the beautiful city of San Francisco. Let me know when you intend to come to New York so we can spend a weekend together. Lucy is dying to see you and is always asking about you and pushing me to write you; but you know that the two of us, meaning you and me, are lazy when it comes to writing.

Well that's enough for today. The cat is rolling over on her back and asking to be petted, and the dog is pawing at me looking for a cookie because she ate all her food and that is her reward if she eats everything.

Write soon and keep well.

Regards,

Dad

As the trolley climbed up Potrero Hill and out of the fog, I sat there in a state of shock. After more than a decade and a half of bachelorhood my dad had finally remarried! That letter and the intimacy it evoked signaled a new beginning in our relationship. Now an adult, I took him up on his invitation and visited him and Lucy whenever I went back East. When my compañera (later wife) Carolyn and I got our doctoral degrees from UMass, Dad and Lucy came to the ceremony to congratulate us. My mother didn't make the trip from Florida, where she was living by then. Years later, when we bought our first home, he and Lucy drove from New York to Minnesota to mark the occasion, and they came bearing a housewarming gift. My mother never came to visit us. Although Dad hadn't been present as a parent, once I reached adulthood, he became a friend to both Carolyn and me.

At age seventy-two, Dad suffered a massive stroke. He was left completely paralyzed, unable to speak, and semicomatose for the next four years. As his condition gradually deteriorated, I occasionally visited him and Lucy at his nursing home in Pennsylvania.

After four years, on a crisp, colorful fall afternoon, the doctors said his end was not far off. As I often do when upset, I took off alone and drove the rural back roads. Listening to the tenor Andrea Bocelli singing "Ave Maria," I was suddenly overcome. I began to weep aloud like I'd never done before in my life, deep, racking sobs. Maybe because Bocelli and I'd shared a common experience of blindness, I'd let my emotional guard down. Music does that sometimes.

I was about to lose the one parent with whom I'd salvaged a civil, almost normal relationship. In her book *Emotional Inheritance* therapist Galit Atlas writes, "Separations are emotional deaths that we have to mourn [because] . . . we always lose more than just the person we love. We lose a life, a future." For years, I'd longed for the love of my absent father, so I wept for me and my dad, and for all our lost time together. After growing up feeling like a motherless child, I was soon to become a fatherless child. Worse, I was about to be left with the burden of dealing with my most difficult surviving parent—alone.

35.   A Deepening Estrangement

FOR A TIME, after Dee was married to my stepfather John, things got better. A tall, quiet former navy MP, John's gift was he was completely devoted to Dee. Since he didn't talk much, I hoped it would give her all the air time and attention she required. But our detente wouldn't last long. When my mother heard of my father's marriage, at first she was in shock, but then her resentment of my rekindled relationship with him and his new wife kicked in. Matters between Dee and me then grew steadily worse.

As my desire for social activism grew, so did my arguments with Dee. Fresh from my stint as a disability activist in San Francisco, I returned to upstate New York. Working in community group homes for people with disabilities, I fancied myself a frontline soldier in the battle for deinstitutionalization and disability rights. But the drudgery of direct service work soon wore me out, and I began looking for work more directly tied to social action.

I eventually ended up at the EOC, where my training and skills as a community organizer took root. But after my abrupt firing from EOC, I spent several months unemployed. Forced to surrender the only apartment I'd ever rented on my own, I became not only homeless but rudderless, jobless, and depressed. After twenty-four long weeks of casting about, I eventually found a position as a community organizer for Citizens Alliance (CA) in Albany, New York. CA was a coalition of unions, churches, tenants' rights groups, and student groups. Having had my fill of housesitting, I could finally afford a place of my own again, but it was a far cry from my earlier spacious third-floor, one-bedroom apartment in trendy downtown Saratoga Springs. All I could afford was a dingy studio apartment that had once been a chicken coop on a farm about six miles north of Saratoga.

Seeking to once again prove myself as an organizer, I became a workaholic, putting in seventy to eighty hours a week at CA fighting downtown gentrification and starting a CA fuel buyers' group. At the time it seemed worth it because my work was being noted and appreciated. I felt I was making a difference again. Leading a state-wide campaign to stop winter utility shutoffs for low- and middle-income families, my CA chapter was chosen to host the main rally at the State Capitol in Albany. I was tasked with organizing about five hundred demonstrators from across New York to pressure legislators to pass the Citizens' Utility Bill of Rights (CUB). For eight weeks, I often worked from 10:00 a.m. to past midnight and would drive back to Saratoga completely spent. I'd then get up at 8:00 a.m. the next morning and begin the routine all over again. Exhausted, but also exhilarated, I saw this as my chance to redeem myself not just in the eyes of fellow progressives but in my own estimation after being fired from EOC.

The night before the Albany rally was to take place, an unexpected late-night call came from Dee. We hadn't been talking and I was fully aware my mother was unfamiliar with and unsupportive of my social justice work. Partially for that reason, I'd not shared the hardship of my months of unemployment and couch hopping with her. When the phone rang, I was sitting alone in the converted chicken coop eating a late-night dinner of cold two-day-old pizza.

Dee began, "I don't want to worry you, but I have to go in for emergency surgery tomorrow. The doctor says I have severe intestinal inflammation, and I have to have part of my colon removed. He feels he has to operate as soon as possible. I need you to come down tomorrow and be here for me." At the time she and John were still living in Queens, about a four-hour drive from Saratoga.

CA was a grassroots nonprofit organization and, as such, was chronically short staffed. As the lead organizer in Albany, I was responsible for the entire rally's logistics—including transportation, publicity, and equipment—and for introducing the speakers.

I couldn't just abandon the rally the night before. Holding the receiver, as I weighed how to tell her I wouldn't get down in time for her operation, my chicken coop of an apartment grew smaller and colder by the second.

Ohh boy, I thought. "Mom," I began, "I can be there in less than twenty-four hours, but tomorrow at noon I'm in charge of a statewide rally. Over five hundred people will be there to stop winter utility shutoffs, and they're counting on me. On this short a notice, there's no one else I can delegate it to. I promise I'll leave directly from Albany as soon as it's over."

Her response was by now expected. "Never mind, if it's too much of a bother. After all, I could die on the operating table, but obviously you could care less. A decent son would come down to be with his mother. But obviously you care more about your precious rally than you do your own mother's life."

I inhaled deeply. Trying not to respond in anger or seem aggrieved, I was about to assure her that I'd be there within the day, but before I could speak she cut me off. "Actually, Jimmy . . ." She paused. "I prefer you don't bother to come down at all." And with that she hung up.

Years later I would learn that Dee regularly fabricated lies to manipulate her friends and strangers to her will. It makes me wonder to this day if she ever had colon surgery. But back then, feeling guilty, manipulated, and cornered, I let my better angels down and decided not to go down to see her. It was a decision I'm not proud of and one I regret to this day. Instead, when the rally resulted in CUB being passed and winter shutoffs being stopped statewide, I threw myself back into my work with renewed gusto.

After the Albany rally it was six months before Dee and I talked again. In the meantime, after work I'd return to the chicken coop late at night and continue drinking and watching TV, alone. Usually, a six pack of beer later, I'd pass out on the moldy secondhand couch. Part of why I was drinking was I was missing a woman I'd been seeing but with whom I'd recently broken up. Partly, I was self-medicating, trying to drown out the little voice that said that I was a Bad Son.

Stephanie Foo in her book *What My Bones Know* says, "I always thought of estrangement as an on–off switch. That's one of the myths, that estrangement is a complete cut off, or it's final." Woo cites Christine Sharp, an associate professor of communications at the University of Washington: "Estrangement is more of a continuum, where you can be more or less estranged, and actually people often go through multiple times of trying to create distance before they're able to maintain a level of distance that's right for them." With Dee, our estrangement never felt liberating, nor did it make me happy. But, as in Woo's experience, it did finally feel necessary.

A decade later and living in Florida, Dee refused to come to my and Carolyn's graduation when we received our doctoral degrees, and later to our wedding. Her stated reason was that John had developed blood clots in his legs and they could no longer fly. Since they'd recently come back from a trip to Hawaii, I suspected the real problem was that I had the gall to invite my father and Lucy to both of those milestone events in my life.

Having my mother removed from my life protected me, but it didn't bring me comfort. But it did clear the way for me to come back into balance. The hardest part was replacing my sense of "family" and finding a place of belonging. Foo suggests the essence of trauma is it makes a person feel like they don't deserve to be loved. The work ahead of me was to rebuild my life so that I could feel loved.

Meanwhile, back in the chicken coop in Saratoga on one especially dark night, burnt out as a community organizer and well into my second six-pack, I found myself calling a substance abuse crisis hotline. Something was about to give.

36.   Wrestling with Moral Outrage

For people who have benefited from the gift of unconditional love, or at least had good parenting, it can be hard to
grasp the terrors a mentally ill parent's behaviors can inflict on a
child. Leslie is a friend and philosophy professor who would help
move my mom into an assisted living center when the time came.
She was also aware that I harbored considerable anger toward Dee.
Over dinner one evening, Leslie wondered whether my mother
should be found not guilty or morally wrong because of her mental
illness. Still, she added, "Your mother is responsible for her behavior because she was an adult woman who didn't seek or didn't have
the opportunity to seek proper mental health care."

Although it was not what Leslie intended, what I heard her say
was my mother should be excused for her behavior. I became so
enraged that I wouldn't speak to Leslie for weeks afterward. She'd
unintentionally touched a raw nerve. When we finally reconnected
at a local pub, I shared my anger in all its glory, beginning with how
I'd been in a cranky mood for weeks after our talk. As we sat across
from one another in our dark wooden booth, I told her how I re-
sented her moral posturing in the face of suffering for which she
had little experience. "I was especially irked because it felt like you
were blithely intellectualizing my relationship with my mother.
For me, your remarks had all the hallmarks of knee-jerk, bleeding-
heart-liberal cluelessness about the suffering of others," I told her.
Apologies to my many liberal friends.

After my rant had run its course, she gulped. "I think I owe you a beer . . . I know I need one," she said, and promptly headed off to the bar to fetch us beers.

To both our credits, that night as the snow fell outside we continued to talk. Sipping our Irish brown ales, Leslie posed a new question, with the caveat that she hoped she wouldn't piss me off again. We were old friends. She asked, "Are you saying mental illness is morally wrong? Or are you saying that if you're mentally ill, choosing parenting is morally wrong?"

At the time I was reading Lori Gottlieb's *Maybe You Should Talk to Someone* with my book group. Pulling it from my backpack, I read Leslie the following passage:

> There's a term we use in therapy: forced forgiveness. Sometimes people feel that in order to get past trauma, they need to forgive whoever caused them the damage—the parent who assaulted them, the burglar that robbed their house, the gang member that killed their son. They're told by well-meaning people that until they can forgive, they'll hold on to the anger. Granted that for some forgiveness can serve as a powerful release. You forgive the person who wronged you, without condoning his actions, and it allows you to move on. But often people feel pressured to forgive and then end up believing something's wrong with them if they can't quite get there, they aren't enlightened enough or strong enough or compassionate enough. So, what I say is this. You can have compassion without forgiving.

"I don't believe mental illness is morally wrong," I said. "But the exception in my mind is those instances that result in physical and/or emotional trauma to others."

Gottlieb suggests 95 percent of parents really want their children to be happy, whether they're doing an A-minus or a D-plus job as parents. Nodding in agreement, Leslie said, "Most parents do the best they can with the resources they've been given." As a single Puerto Rican mother in New York amid the racism of the 1970s, my mother clearly had few resources with which to cope with her own history of trauma.

In order to be heard over the sound of the bar's Trivial Pursuit contest, I was forced to speak louder. "The question is, what do I do with that?" Not breaking eye contact, Leslie leaned back into the booth and took another sip of her beer as I grabbed a handful of stale popcorn.

I said, "Eventually, the place that I think I've gotten to with my mother for now is one of compassion. It was what it was, and no amount of wishing it had been different changes what was. I don't forgive the knife, the closet, or the other emotionally abusive behaviors. But I now accept that Dee's actions were probably a result of her trauma and resulting mental illness. Nevertheless, they felt morally wrong to me. If child abuse can't be classified as immoral, I guess I don't know what can be."

Leslie asked, "Should people with mental illness then be allowed to have children?"

Munching on the salty popcorn, I said, "I can't know what my life would have been like with a different mother, what kind of person I might have become, or if I would've had a life at all. And I have no idea who would possibly be in a position to judge a parent's mental fitness to have children."

As we finished our beers and were putting on coats, I added, "It's not the case for everyone equally yet, but I'm just thankful that more treatments are available today than in my mother's lifetime." I smiled. "Leslie, keep buying me those beers and asking questions. It's complex, and forgiveness is an ongoing dilemma I'm working on. Your questions help me go deeper as I try to get clearer." But the question about whether Dee should have had a child, and whether I should forgive her continued to haunt me.

Many years later I would run across an idea that resonated deeply with my dilemma about whether to forgive Dee:

Consider replacing the word "forgive" with the word "release." In other words, instead of forgiving people, you're releasing them. You're releasing them from your life so they no longer have a hold on you. Simply change the question from "How do I forgive them?" to "How do I release them?"

And then consider yourself, love yourself, value yourself, and know you have the power to change the dynamics of any situation.

—Anita Moorjani

This distinction between forgiving and releasing felt right to me. However, the moment when I could finally "release" Dee from my life would not come to pass for many years.

37. Why Choose Dee as a Parent?

MY CONVERSATION WITH LESLIE had gotten me thinking and writing about Dee. After I read a draft of the following chapter to my writers' group, one person opined, "Children don't get to choose their parents." Yet I'd heard several spiritual mediums, people who explore past lives, say something quite to the contrary. I shared with the book group what one psychic medium once told me. "Children choose their parents in this reincarnation to learn particular lessons they need in order to become more spiritually evolved," the medium suggested.

This caused the group to pause and then engendered a slew of interesting comments. Some didn't believe in past lives. Some felt like it was akin to blaming victims for their abuse. Others thought it worth contemplating. I said, "When I first heard what the medium said about choosing one's parents, I said to myself, 'Well that's just ridiculous! Why would I have chosen a mother who chased me with a knife? What, am I crazy too?'"

But the more I thought about it, if nothing more than as an exercise in creative thinking, the more reasons I came up with to consider the idea worthy of consideration. I came up with a list of eight possibilities for why I might have chosen Dee as my mother in this life.

1. Dee, by virtue of her sheer tenacity and fierceness, imprinted on me a sense of survival and perseverance against all odds.

2. Her determined efforts to find a "cure" for my blindness succeeded where perhaps a lesser personality would have failed.

3. She was a force of nature and I had to learn to stand up to my mother, even when it caused me emotional pain and alienation.

4. Her inability to nurture a supportive family environment forced me to seek my own family outside the boundaries of traditional family.

5 Her struggles with her mental health illuminated for me the need to develop and nurture mechanisms to preserve and heal my own psychic wounds.

6. Her propensity for harsh judgment and inability to practice forgiveness and gratitude jolted me into seeing similar tendencies in myself. As a result, I took up meditation to counteract some of these weaknesses in myself.

7. Her internalized racism, especially toward fellow Puerto Ricans, was the start of my reclaiming a positive, affirming Nuyorican sense of self. It also jump-started my commitment to social justice work.

8. I continue to grapple with my inherited tendency to, once offended, hold onto grudges. Watching as this tendency eroded my mother's circle of family and friends over many years has, I hope, alerted me to its shortsightedness.

The idea forced me to consider this question: *Could a kinder, gentler, more nurturing parent have taught me as well?* Maybe not.

In many ways Dee was a very smart woman who, being a single, Puerto Rican mother, had the deck stacked against her. Unfortunately, at times she projected her anger and frustrations onto her only child. That's part of the reason why I found it was easier to idealize my father, who was distant for so many years, than my ever-present yet troubled mother. In his book *Tasha: A Son's Memoir*, Brian Morton says, "Just as no man is a hero to his valet, few mothers are heroes to their sons." In acknowledging my outrage at her abusive outbursts, I'm forced to acknowledge that Dee was more than her mental illness. She was a Latina working-class single mother raising a child with a disability in an era of limited opportunities for smart Puerto Rican women.

Yet Dee could also be the life of any party. Her bubbly, buoyant personality would emerge, and she'd laugh and dance the night away. She loved nothing more than getting dressed up and going out to dances sponsored by the Knights of Columbus. Sometimes, with no date, she would take me to weddings and get me up to salsa dance, publicly complimenting me on what a good dancer I was. One of her lasting gifts to me was imparting the love and confidence to dance in social settings.

I was often confused when my mother would make herself the brunt of jokes. For years I'd be embarrassed when she'd mispronounce the words "sheets" and "beach," instead uttering "shits" and "bitch." In my teens, it finally dawned on me that she didn't do it as a mistake, but to solicit laughter by making fun of her Puerto Rican accent. Using laughter, she gained social acceptance and blunted White folks' racist discomfort about her being Puerto Rican.

The Park Avenue surgeon who eventually performed the cutting-edge cataract surgery on my right eye was world-famous. The waiting list to see him was years long. Using her *Long Island Press* connections, somehow my mother was able to get me to the front of the line. This was her most enduring gift to me.

Six years earlier, when I was fourteen, she learned that *Parade* magazine sponsored a contest for newspaper boys from around the country for a chance to win a trip to Europe. Again, because of her newspaper connections, I spent an incredible two weeks in Spain and Portugal in 1968. I'm not even sure I had a newspaper route at that time.

That trip instilled a deep love of travel in me, partly because it embodied the best moments of our relationship. Posing as a reporter who worked for the *Long Island Press*, she'd finagle us other free trips, including bus tours to Washington, DC, and Pennsylvania

Dutch country. Once she even landed us a free cruise to the Bahamas. Although her secretary's salary was limited, by charming her male bosses she afforded me opportunities that were unimaginable to children from most single-parent households.

Part of her charm was her extroverted personality. She could strike up a conversation with total strangers. Her combination of good looks and humor enabled her to make friends wherever she went. Sadly, her quick temper lost her as many friends as she gained, but her gift of gab was a trait she passed on to her only child.

Dee's buoyant spirit was most keenly on display at Christmas. One of my most pleasant childhood memories is how she managed to get us front-row seats at the reviewing stand for the annual Macy's Thanksgiving Day Parade. Every year she'd get press passes so I could see Santa up close as the parade ended—especially important to a kid with limited vision. Afterward, we'd go for lunch to the famous Horn & Hardart automat on Times Square. For less than two dollars we could enjoy a large, although bland, meal purchased from shining glass display cases. She'd give me quarters so I could approach the cashier by myself to exchange them for gold tokens. Those tokens allowed us to pick out our meals from the display, where you'd insert the tokens into a slot. Each stack of glass-doored dispensers had a rotating metal cylinder. I was mesmerized by how an array of pies (chocolate, apple, and cherry) would magically appear like a carousel before your eyes in the case. I'd excitedly insert my token and turn the brass knob, and the glass door would pop open so I could remove my chosen pie.

Full on lunch and pie, we'd stroll Park Avenue to gawk at the animated window holiday displays at Saks Fifth Avenue and the Macy's flagship store. We'd watch through frozen breath and listen as the stores piped out Christmas carols into the street. Our last stop was always Rockefeller Center. The smells of hot pretzels and roasted chestnuts were everywhere. There we'd rub elbows with crowds of onlookers pointing to the colorfully dressed ice skaters doing graceful spins and leaps below the sixty-foot Rockefeller Plaza Christmas tree.

In our tiny apartment in Forest Hills on Christmas Eve, I'd fall asleep under the watchful glow of my brightly lit red-and-white plastic Santa Claus. When I'd wake in the morning, our artificial tree was magically transformed and a half dozen presents awaited my attention. To my astonishment, the cold milk and chocolate chip cookies we'd left for Santa the night before were always consumed. Since our tree was in the bedroom, how Santa managed to slip by me unseen was always part of the mystery. This savoring of the Christmas spirit survived Dee, and today my wife and I continue our own Christmas traditions of decorating and hosting Día de los Reyes fiestas for friends. And I still bring out my fifty-year-old Santa Claus nightlight for the holidays.

Unfortunately, her buoyant spirit and ability to make friends easily and quickly could never quite keep pace with her explosive temper, excessively judgmental nature, narcissism, and unforgiving attitude toward others. Over time I noticed that people with whom she'd grown initially close would fall away. First friends from the *Long Island Press,* then from their retirement community in upstate New York, and finally even her stepchildren would shun her. In later years, her stable of close friends shrank until she had none left in her orbit. Long-term friends and family were replaced by casual acquaintances she'd meet and charm at the senior citizen complex she inhabited in Coral Springs, Florida. This social isolation, followed by the trauma surrounding the death of John, would soon cause her dormant PTSD and other mental illness to reemerge.

38. Temagami Vision Quest

In 1980, after being fired from EOC, I was in a sad way. Luckily, one of the guys in my first men's group was a staffer at Sagamore Lodge in Raquette Lake, New York. Situated in the midst of upstate New York's majestic Adirondack Mountains, Sagamore was originally the summer home of Alfred Vanderbilt, one of America's original robber barons. Now listed on the National Register of Historic Places, Sagamore was converted into a conference center that hosts workshops and outdoor getaways. Thanks to my friend, I was offered a summer internship where, in return for room and board, I washed dishes, led nature hikes, and guided paddling trips on Sagamore's private lake. Jobless, and without a place of my own, I found the retreat into the Adirondacks was a fortuitous coincidence and consistent with my seeking solace in wild places. Little did I know just how fortuitous.

One of Sagamore's workshops was being led by Rod Napier, a noted figure in the team-building and human potential movement. Over dinner, Rod spoke of a three-week vision quest program he was organizing in the remote Temagami Lakes region of northeastern Ontario, Canada. "This place is so remote participants will have to take a bush plane just to get to the island base camp," he said.

Since I'd read all of Carlos Castaneda's books, I knew a little about vision questing. And being an admirer of Native American cultures, I was taken with the idea.

"This being the first year and therefore a pilot program, I'm handpicking this year's participants," Rod added.

"Man, that sounds like the trip of a lifetime," I said.

Rod smiled. "Why don't you come along?"

"Yeah, right," I cracked. "I couldn't afford the price of the bush plane ride, never mind the expense of the whole program."

Over the course of his week at Sagamore, Rod had learned of my outdoor skills, my lifeguard certification, and that I'd been legally blind. Nevertheless, I was gobsmacked when he said, "Well, maybe we just have to provide you with a scholarship. It'll be useful to have a person with your skills and life experience in the party."

Eight weeks later, I found myself aboard a Cessna 185 amphibious seaplane circling the Temagami base camp with three other participants. Our plane made a jarring landing on the lake and then slowly taxied to the dock. Disembarking, I noticed sixty loons in a flock (called an "asylum") at the far end of the lake. I've always been taken by loons and their eerily evocative calls, but I'd never seen more than three in one place before. I took it as a good omen.

We spent the next two days learning about wilderness survival and practicing our canoeing skills. On the third day, a group of six canoes with twelve people set off for a ten-day wilderness and team-building experience. Joining Rod and our two guides on the trip was a Native American shaman named Elizabeth Cogburn. Elizabeth fit none of my stereotyped images of what a Native American shaman was supposed to look like. Not only was she female (yeah, I hear my sexism), she was a tall, gray- and blond-haired woman in her early sixties from Albuquerque, New Mexico. I confess I was skeptical.

During the next ten days we were blessed by viewings of the Northern Lights, bald eagles, a black bear, and even a cow moose with her calf. Sleeping under the night sky, the stars shone as brilliantly as those at New York's Hayden Planetarium, except these were the real deal! As we lay on the shore in our sleeping bags, one of the guides pointed to a passing satellite, bright yellow against the ebony sky. It was the first satellite I'd ever been able to see with my one restored eye. Bathed in awe, seeing stars like I'd never seen before, I fell asleep to the call of loons.

Our trip was not without its frightening moments. A Latina participant, who had earlier admitted she didn't know how to swim, also confessed she'd considered suicide. On our eighth day out, she tried to drown herself by jumping off a ledge into deep water. Alone and reading in my tent, I was unaware of what was unfolding until shouting drew me to the shoreline. Fortunately, my Water Safety Instructor and CPR skills were not called upon, as one of the other participants swam out and pulled her to safety.

Watching, a memory flashed into my mind's eye of my mother. Nervously, I chuckled at the idea that maybe the omen of the "asylum" hadn't been just an idle figure of speech. Later that evening, in my journal I wrote that perhaps the message for me was that like this woman, my mother wasn't my responsibility to save. Writing those words left me with alternating states of relief, guilt, shame, and liberation.

Upon our return to base camp, Elizabeth began the serious preparations for our solo vision quest experiences. This involved undergoing a sweat lodge ceremony for purification and then paddling at least a mile away to a remote location. Elizabeth said the exact location for our quest "Would choose us." *Well, that's not helpful*, I thought. Once there, we were instructed to flip our red canoes over so that they'd be visible from the air. This was in the event that if we didn't return as scheduled, a search party would know where to begin. I was to spend three days and nights alone in the Canadian wilderness. While there, I would ritually fast and sleep in a circle of protection, which I'd been shown how to fashion using tobacco.

I recall little of that time, as we weren't permitted to bring journals or books. It rained constantly, and I was bored and tired much of the time. What I do recall is lying in my sleeping bag covered in plastic as the rain beat down mercilessly on my exposed face. I had to laugh at the absurdity of it all. On my final morning, the sun finally broke through the cloud cover. Sitting up, I was more than a little disappointed that no major visions or inspirations had come to me. Hungry and looking forward to a hot breakfast back at camp, I crawled out of my bag and stood. Looking out over the fog-laden lake, I greeted the nearby white pines with a bow. That's when I noticed a large pile of fresh wolf scat just outside the ring of protection in which I'd spent the night. It had definitely not been there the day before. A feeling of excitement and dread simultaneously coursed through my veins. Nervously checking over my shoulder,

I quickly picked up my things and hastily clambered over ancient granite boulders down to my canoe. Flipping my canoe upright, I took one final glance back as I paddled through the morning mist back to camp.

That evening featured a light feast to break our fast, celebrate, and give thanks that all participants had returned safely. Gathered around the dining hall's rough-hewn table, we shared our vision quest stories one by one. Just as I finished telling of my close encounter with a curious wolf, from somewhere across the darkened lake a lone wolf let out a solitary howl. A standing Elizabeth declared, "This is a sign that our relative the Wolf has come to join us in our Closing Circle."

At midnight, Elizabeth organized a campfire for a Circle Dance. Accompanied by two drummers, twelve people danced, at first alone, then together, throughout the night. Hours later, as dawn's first gray light began to chase away the coal black darkness, Elizabeth led us into a tighter and tighter circle. Finally, we found ourselves corkscrewed into the center, forming a body-hugging helix. "This circle represents our interconnections with Mother Earth, our fellow human beings, and the Great Spirit. It is a symbolic recreation of the ancient Spiral of Life," she sang out from the center.

Even after I'd completed my vision quest, I was still not 100 percent bought into what I'd labeled Elizabeth's "woo-woo" rituals. But as our circle collapsed in on itself, from across the misty waters first one, then a chorus of wolves filled the chilly morning air with their howls. With a motion of her hand Elizabeth stopped the drummers, and we all froze. My moment of skepticism evaporated like an ice cube sizzling in a hot skillet.

Whispering from the center of the helix, she said, "Brother Wolf has come to bless us and to say goodbye. Let us be grateful."

Later, as I stowed my backpack aboard the pontoon plane for our return flight, a single loon appeared and paddled toward the dock. It being late September, most of the "asylum" had since departed for their overwintering waters in the Atlantic Ocean. Turning away from the plane, I silently wished this lone loon well. Then aloud I said, "Time for you to begin your pilgrimage, friend."

Or was that the loon speaking through me? As if on cue, it let out a tremulous yodel, turned, and slowly lifted off the lake, headed in a southeasterly direction toward the Atlantic coast. Grateful to the loon and for the clarity of the moment, I realized that Mother Earth was letting me know that my quest for vision was just beginning, and yet again that I was never alone.

39. Uncle Bim

> Days pass and the years vanish and
> we walk sightless among miracles.
> —REFORM JEWISH SHABBAT PRAYER

AFTER EOC I HIT ROCK BOTTOM ... hard. In Saratoga I'd been seeing a lovely woman named Michelle with two young children, Vanessa who was five and Joey who was seven. Ours had been a passionate romance, Michelle, a poet, and me, a community organizer. After my unemployment ran out, we decided to throw in together, and I moved in with her. It was a kind of instant family. I reveled in taking the kids for their first-ever visit to the ocean and teaching them to bodysurf on the Jersey Shore. At Christmas, I bought the family used cross-country skis and took us to Sagamore Lodge for a free winter wonderland weekend. Sagamore and I had a previous connection from my years of interning there and helping train their volunteers.

As we became more serious, Michelle and I went to a couples' retreat weekend at Sagamore. Sadly, that's when the fantasy of "instant family" began to crumble. She had her babies very young, starting at seventeen. She was an excellent mother and suitably protective. I, on the other hand, was a self-absorbed twentysomething ideologue with little appreciation for the patience and sacrifice required to be a parent. One day, I became overly frustrated by the kids' and Michelle's habit of throwing their dirty laundry down the basement stairs. I routinely stumbled over it as I'd take my own dirty clothes to do a laundry. Finally, after slipping and falling half-way down the staircase, I made a tactless decision. I posted a sign on the cellar door that read:

DO NOT THROW CLOTHES DOWN THE STAIRS!

Talk about the house guest from hell! Unfortunately, that incident was the beginning of the end. Michelle explained in no uncertain terms that this was her house and I was not welcome to post signs. It was only years later that I came to understand that having just one good eye, and my subsequent lack of depth perception, made it inevitable that I'd not see the clothes as I climbed downstairs.

Meanwhile, Joan and Steven, two pals from my Camp Lighthouse days and later Camp Jened, lived in Amherst, Massachusetts, about three hours from Saratoga. I made a trip to visit them, and Steven told me of an amazing graduate program in social justice education at UMass.

"With your background as an organizer, you'd be an ideal candidate," he said.

No one in my immediate family besides me had ever attended college, never mind gone to graduate school. I smiled and put the idea out of my mind.

After the EOC debacle and months of being unemployed, I finally landed a community organizing job with Citizens Alliance, where I routinely worked ridiculously long hours. Michelle, tiring of my absence and my ineptitude as a coparent, one night kindly suggested we separate. No longer living with Michelle's family, I developed my regular habit of polishing off six-packs of beer to decompress in my chicken coop.

The night I drunkenly called a suicide helpline turned out to be a sufficient intervention to shake me out of my miasma. I decided soon after to move to Amherst to live with Joan and Steven while I established my residency for graduate school.

Two months before I moved into their home, they had their first child, Elena. Our agreement was I'd live with them rent-free and in exchange, I'd provide "Elie-Care" two nights a week. So that's how I became a "manny." It's where I learned about changing diapers, patience, and experiencing unconditional love. It was my first real nuclear family experience.

When she was young, Elie couldn't pronounce "Jim," so instead she called me "Uncle Bim." After four years together with Joan, Steven, and Elie, I eventually met and began living with my future life companion, Carolyn. We soon graduated together from UMass with our doctorates, and I commenced a forty-year career in social justice education as a professor and consultant.

My education in community and family—first begun at Camp Lighthouse, then at Dover Environmental Center, then with Michelle and the kids—continued with Joan, Steven, Elie, and, later, Elie's younger brother Micah. For the first time, I began considering the possibility of finding family of my own. But what was to become of my estranged relationship with Dee?

40. Redefining Machismo

THE IDEA TO START a Latino men's group sprang from my college experience back at Cortland with my first "rap group" and, later, my first men's group in Saratoga. Being an only child, I grew up with no brothers and sisters. The idea grew from my need to connect with Latino brothers in the overwhelmingly Anglo town of Amherst, Massachusetts. As a Puerto Rican man, I'd begun reading and paying attention to the voices of women of color who were challenging not only the racism and sexism of men, but that of the White women's movement as well. Latina writers like Cherríe Moraga, Gloria Anzaldúa, and Aurora Levins Morales were giving voice to the unique experiences, concerns, and perspectives of women of color living with racism and sexism. These writers were trying to create a new, broader, and more inclusive women's movement. But as a Puerto Rican man, I had to first unlearn my unconscious sexism in order to take these women's voices to heart.

A movement of men was awakening to our complicity in a social order that systematically undervalues women while often overvaluing the contributions of men. This was where I began to understand how I unknowingly colluded with sexism and the price men pay, emotionally and physically, for hanging on to the unearned privilege of entitlement.

Back in Saratoga, I wondered why I could not fully identify with the White men struggling to be allies to women. Why didn't I feel able to completely throw myself into the struggle to end sexism as defined by the emerging (White) men's movement?

The answer seemed to lie with the overwhelmingly White, middle-class nature of the men's movement. When I joined my first men's group in Saratoga Springs, terms that were freely thrown about to describe sexism—*Casanova, Don Juan, machismo, Latin lover*—seemed to only distance me from my roots. Not only were all these men White, they used terms that implied that "true sexism" was associated with being Latino.

The criticism of traditional "machismo" with its rigid sex role stereotypes (*you aren't a real man unless you earn more than your wife*) and its double standards (*men can have mistresses, women must stay devoted*) made little sense to me. My experience in the Anglo world showed that this behavior was not unique to Latinos, but I wondered what it might be like to engage with other Latino men in addressing both sexism and racism as we explored our identities.

So at thirty, I helped organize my first men's group composed of just Latinos. The experience was both deeply disturbing and enormously satisfying. Five of us met at Casa Latina, a community agency serving Latin@s in western Massachusetts. We were Puertorriqueños and Dominicanos. Initially we weren't sure of what to talk about. Yet to be together just felt right, so we continued to meet for bimonthly tertulias (discussions) over café.

Our initial meetings became a process of feeling each other out. How safe would it be? Could we trust our own kind to not put us down? We only half-joked about the old saying that when Latinos assemble a firing squad, we do it in a circle. I understand now this was our way of saying, "Mira, if I open up here don't shoot me down, OK?" Thus, we began to tentatively explore our differences as Latinos, as men, and as hermanos.

Some of us came from working-class or poor economic backgrounds. Some had run with gangs, been in trouble with the law, or struggled mightily to survive hostile classrooms and racist teachers. To our surprise we discovered that several of us had been placed in classrooms for kids with "disabilities." That was one way that Anglo teachers had dealt with our differences. It was only years later that we would realize that we never had a disability, other than the disabling effects of negative teacher stereotypes.

Others had grown up in middle-class families in their native countries. Their experiences had been mostly free of racism or forced assimilations. El Grupo, as we called ourselves, became a place to recount our rage at North America's racism. As the weeks and months passed, El Grupo became a space for rediscovering what it meant to be Latino, and male, in America. Over the course of two years, we explored our various identities, language differences, bicultural relationships, sexism, and machismo. We made linkages between racism and sexism in ways that had been impossible for me in my earlier White men's groups.

Part of this process meant confronting our internalized oppression and dealing with what Eldridge Cleaver, in *Soul on Ice*, called, ofay women. These were the blond, blue-eyed "ideals" who haunted our romantic fantasies and simultaneously separated us from Latinas in our lives. One of our gay hermanos even joked of an earlier lover being an "ofay boy." That was my first tertulia with gay and bisexual Latinos. We were more different than we thought. We are more similar than we imagined.

I helped co-organize two more Latino men's groups in the years to come. Our umbrella of Latinos would come to include Cubanos, Mexicanos, Chicanos, and Colombianos. Initially there were questions about being too diverse, but again and again, we'd both recognize our diversity and be struck by our commonalities. We included Latinos who'd experienced very little oppression and some who ran into it headfirst every day. Yet we found that we all struggled with internalized oppression.

Our discussions about racism within the Latino community were hard, but also illuminating. Within families, brothers and sisters spanned the range from light-skinned (blanquitos) to toffee colored (café con leche) to Black (morenos). While we came to understand the subtle racism of these distinctions, we were also a living, breathing challenge to North America's obsession with race as merely Black or White.

Over time we came to laugh at the old joke about circular firing squads. El Grupo showed us that our differences did not have to be a source of division. They helped us understand the fullness of what it meant to be Latino in a way that strengthened our sense of community. Thanks to El Grupo, I came to see that our differences need not splinter us. I learned that my obsession with blond, blue-eyed Anglas was not an isolated phenomenon, but a form of systemic and internalized racism. I was forced to reevaluate standards of beauty taught by an Anglo value system that denied the beauty of my own family.

Our group came to trust and support one another as men who were learning to undo the shackles of oppression while refraining from adding to the oppression of others. We learned that we could set aside the oppressive vestiges of machismo and also create a new machismo—being man enough to be an ally to women as well as to gays, lesbians, and bisexuals within and outside our community.

It was sometimes discomforting. We could say things and hear things from one another that we would not or could not hear from outsiders. We came to understand the varied lessons our fathers taught us about being men, some of which we continued to embrace, and others we tried to change, or chose to reject.

In the end, I recognized that as a Latino I have as great a responsibility to point out sexist behavior as I do to criticize Anglos for their racist behavior. Each form of oppression—racism, sexism, heterosexism, classism, ableism—diminishes us by tearing at the fabric that binds us as a community—respecto. In redefining what it meant to be Latino, I learned that I could celebrate my culture at the same time as I critiqued it. By disclosing our fears, we discovered that we became more fully who we wanted to be.

41. Dee's Last Act

IT WAS 11:00 P.M. and the phone rang. Carolyn and I were already in bed. In the dark I groped for the phone on our bedside table.

"James, there's been an incident. Your mother is all right, but she's brandishing a knife in the presence of one of our staff. Because she's threatening to harm herself we were forced to call the police. They will be transporting her by ambulance to the hospital."

It had only been one month since we'd moved Dee and all her belongings to Minnesota up from Florida. In that time, we found her an apartment in a nearby assisted living facility.

I made the fifteen-minute drive from our farmhouse in St. Peter to North Mankato in under nine minutes. But by the time I got there the police had left and Dee had been whisked away. The staff and I searched the little apartment to see whether there was any more cutlery Dee might have stashed away. The director of the facility was a kindly woman who originally suggested we pick the apartment opposite her office. "I can keep a closer eye on Dinorah that way," she'd offered. That evening, the director beckoned my wife and me across the hall into her office.

Closing the door so as not to be overheard, she said, "Given your mom's rapid deterioration and potential to harm herself and maybe others, we can no longer accommodate her in our assisted living unit. I recommend you consider moving her into the memory care unit as soon as a room becomes available."

The memory care unit was the locked wing of the facility designed specifically for residents suffering disorientation, Alzheimer's, dementia, and other illnesses requiring 24/7 monitoring. Carolyn and I exchanged glances. A month earlier back in Florida doctors told us Dee had a brain tumor that was massive and growing quickly. After showing us the MRI scan of her brain, a neurosurgeon who looked like Marcus Welby asked, "You understand that your mother's condition is terminal?"

On the plane down to Florida, I'd guessed the outlook was bad and prepared myself for the worst. Yet the words that the person who brought me into the world was shortly to leave it caught me by surprise. Sitting in the small beige examination room, I felt my vision narrow into a small periscope. All I could see was the neurosurgeon's face, and all I could hear was my own breathing. I surmised this was not the first time he was telling an adult child to prepare for a mother's imminent passing. I was comforted that his face reflected a kindness I hadn't expected in a state psychiatric facility. In a weak voice, I asked, "How long?"

Nodding, the doctor said, "Hard to be exact, but I guess it's a matter of weeks, maybe two or three months at most."

Since her prognosis was grim, we hoped to keep Dee as independent as possible for as long as possible. We moved all her furniture from Florida to Minnesota hoping to create as familiar a setting as humanly feasible. We'd toured the facility's memory care unit. It consisted of three wings with the nursing station at the hallway's crossroads. The rooms were small bedrooms with a bathroom, no kitchen, and no living room. It meant that Dee would be surrounded by the unfamiliar, a terrifying prospect for a person already suffering the disorienting effects of dementia caused by a brain tumor.

Carolyn was the first to ask, "This means that unless a room becomes open in your memory care unit, we'll have to move her to a different facility?" The director nodded.

In Florida, Dee had first been institutionalized in a state psych unit only one month ago. She had shown up at the local emergency room with a gun, disoriented and threatening to harm herself. It'd been a massive three-day production to move her out of her small Hollywood, Florida, apartment and find a temporary assisted living unit nearby while we scouted for a place for her in Minnesota. Somehow Carolyn and I had gotten it all done. It took under a week to pack up her little apartment, arrange an apartment at Minnesota's Oak Terrace assisted living facility, and then find a company to move all her belongings from Florida.

We hired a facilitator in Florida who specialized in these kinds of crises for the aged. It was money well spent. But the idea of now moving her to a fourth different place seemed out of the question. Unlike in Florida, the options for southern Minnesota's elderly are far more limited. Besides, the Oak Terrace staff in Mankato had proven fantastic. Despite being underpaid and understaffed, these working-class White women were, on the whole, remarkably compassionate as well as capable. It was my mom's favorite aide, Cindy, who had talked Dee into surrendering the steak knife just before the police arrived. Nevertheless, Dee was taken to the psychiatric ward of the local Mayo hospital.

I arrived at the hospital just in time to sit in on her intake evaluation with the psychiatrist on call. Because she was already agitated, and her doctor was a dark-skinned Pakistani man, Dee proved uncooperative. At one point he asked her to tell him the date, and she irritably replied, "Really, doctor, you seem an intelligent man. I shouldn't have to tell you it's 1975." The actual date was September 28, 2010.

His next question made me squirm in my chair. "And who is this man sitting next to you?" First looking to me then back to him, she replied, "My God, this is my husband of course!" I took a deep swallow, but I was totally creeped out.

Dee remained in an uncooperative mood, so they decided to hold her overnight in an unlocked wing adjacent to the psychiatric unit. The next day a young Nepali intern rotated in, but Dee refused to answer any of his questions. In the middle of her interview with him she got up and walked out into the hallway in search of her clothes. "These people are idiots!" she shouted. "I'm leaving."

Because the secured part of the psych unit was overcrowded, she hadn't yet been assigned a bed within the locked unit. This posed a problem on many levels. One was I had no desire to wrestle an angry 230-pound Puerto Rican woman back into her room. Alerted by the doctor, the charge nurse, a petite Mexican American woman, appeared in the hall next to a fuming Dee.

She stepped alongside Dee and said calmly in Spanish, "I'd love to hear about Puerto Rico, Dinorah. I've never been, but my husband and I are planning a trip there. Would you be willing to sit with me in the lounge and give me some tips for a first-time visitor?"

Her pride restored and not forced to go to her room against her will, my mother gratefully accepted the charge nurse's invitation. Sensing my concern, the nurse turned to me. "I think we'll be fine now. Why don't you go out and come back later after she's had her dinner?"

When we returned two hours later we found Dee sedated and sleeping happily. In the meantime, I'd heard back from Oak Terrace. A room in their memory unit would be available the very next day. This was Oak Terrace code for "A resident has just died, which has freed up a bed."

The hospice nurse assigned to Dee's case proved to be an astonishing human being. A middle-aged woman with untamed naturally red hair, Kathleen took me aside to a small coffee lounge behind the nurse's station. Sitting me down, she slowly poured me a cup of coffee.

"Your mother is bright, but highly manipulative. And she's going to try and work you at every opportunity. It's her only means of controlling her situation," she said matter-of-factly.

I leaned against the orange plastic chair's backrest for support. "You can tell all that after only one visit? How is it possible you figured her out so soon?"

Pushing back an unruly gray lock from her otherwise red mane, Kathleen smiled and patted my shoulder. A heavyset woman, she had an aura of Irish beauty. "Honey, I've been doing this for thirty-one years. Mothers and the trips they run on their sons is nothing new to me. My guess? She's going to lie to make her situation seem even more pitiful. That way you'll have to give her all your attention. You need to understand she's in no pain. Don't be pulled into her melodrama."

Feeling a need to explain (or be exonerated?), I said, "Kathleen, I'll be coming on Mondays, Tuesdays, and Fridays and on weekends since my job is up in the Twin Cities. Carolyn will cover Wednesdays and Thursdays when I'm at work."

Nodding sympathetically, Kathleen said, "That'll be plenty, but she'll still make a fuss. Don't get fooled. It doesn't make any difference if you're here 24/7. It still won't ever be enough for her."

"That's been the story of my life with Dee! You don't realize what a huge weight you've taken off my shoulders," I sighed. My neck muscles unknotted for the first time since the melodrama began weeks ago.

Tucking a stray lock back behind her ear, Kathleen added, "I'm guessing the whole pulling-the-knife episode was an act to get you down here."

Sitting opposite this hospice angel I was completely in awe. In her one-hour intake, Kathleen had grasped what it'd taken me years of counseling to get my head around. After years of therapy, and with Kathleen's external validation, I was forced to accept that Dee was an insecure, highly emotional, anxious, manipulative, and narcissistic personality. She'd lied and manufactured scenes to get her way since her childhood.

My esteem for hospice nurses going through the roof, I asked, "Kathleen, where have you been all my life? You could've saved me a fortune in therapy bills." Her green eyes sparkling, Kathleen let out a hearty laugh. "Yeah, I hear that a lot."

After Dee was discharged from the psych unit and back at Oak Terrace, the next five weeks passed by quietly. As predicted, her condition deteriorated quickly. She was talking less and seemed more and more disoriented.

One morning at 5:00 a.m., we were awakened by the ringing of the bedside phone. Dee had been found lying on the bathroom floor after falling in the middle the night. They'd taken her to the hospital again. I made it to the hospital just as an emergency room doctor began to stitch her bleeding head. The image is seared into my memory. The experience of consoling a sobbing Dee as she received four stitches on her scalp was not unlike holding the hand of a frightened five-year-old in pain. From that night forward, Dee's bed was fitted with an alarm so that staff could be alerted to any late-night wanderings or trips to the toilet.

There came a point in late October when Dee stopped talking altogether. Only once did she swim up from her mental fog: It was the visit when I brought her one of her old photo albums. Judging by the sepia photographs and yellowed pages, the album had to be at least sixty years old. Dee instantly became alert and animated. Pointing, she named everyone in the photos in a loud and clear voice. But it was the last day the world would hear Dee's voice. Afterward, she retreated back into herself and seemed to not recognize Carolyn or me. Ironically for me, her vision would also soon diminish to the point of complete blindness.

In November Kathleen informed us it was unlikely my mother would make it to Christmas. So a few weeks before Thanksgiving, Carolyn and I decorated her room with colorful holiday lights. Since Dee had always loved Christmas, we decided, *What the hell. Let's give her one more Christmas light show.*

The call we'd been expecting came at 7:45 a.m. A hollow sensation spread across my chest as I reached over and picked up the bedside phone. Her favorite aide, Cindy, had come to dress Dee, who after not eating for the past five days had been in a coma.

On the phone Cindy explained, "Suddenly Dee sat up in her bed, opened her eyes wide, and raised both arms as if reaching out for an unseen visitor. She then lay back, closed her eyes, and was gone."

In the time it took for us to arrive, the staff had changed her soiled bedclothes, combed her hair, and pulled a thin blue sheet up to her chin. Except for her ashen pallor, Dee seemed asleep, but I could sense her Spirit had departed the room. The holiday lights, having been left on overnight, imparted a note of melancholy to the scene. Waiting for the undertaker to arrive, Carolyn and I closed our eyes and sat and meditated over Dee's body. We asked her Spirit to not be afraid. It was unusually quiet on the floor, and even with my eyes closed, I felt a Light entering the space and imparting an impression of calm and comfort.

Moments later a quiet knocking on the door signaled that the funeral director from St. Peter had arrived. I'd met with him weeks earlier to make the cremation arrangements. After they gave me a moment to stroke her hair, kiss her forehead, and say "I love you" one last time, we stepped outside so he and his assistant could move her body onto their gurney. As her shrouded body was wheeled out of the room and past us, the poignancy of the moment hit me. That was the last time I'd ever see Dee in her corporeal form. I'd spent much of my life wrestling with whether or not I could love her. In this moment I felt I had found resolution. Before exiting the room, I reached down and unplugged her Christmas lights.

In the months since her first hospitalization, I had lost twenty pounds. Now, perhaps not surprisingly, for the first time since her torment began I felt at peace. Her (and our) ordeal was over. Wordlessly holding hands, Carolyn and I walked out of Oak Terrace for the last time.

In the car Carolyn turned to me and said, "You know we did a good job, a really good job. And you were a really good son."

As we sat together in the front seat, taking in our newfound freedom, I thanked Carolyn. With Oak Terrace receding in the rearview mirror, I whispered, "It only took fifty-five years, but I can finally say, without a tinge of shame, I am a good son."

42. Riding the Waves

Occasionally, Mother Earth teaches a lesson we can only recognize with the benefit of 20/20 hindsight. In my case it took decades before I was able to fully grasp Her role in guiding my Spiritual journey.

I learned to bodysurf when I was about ten at Jones Beach, New York. Few activities in the outdoors gave me as much joy as riding the waves in rough surf. The bigger the waves, the greater the thrill, alongside the risk of being tossed like a ragdoll and crushed against the ocean's floor. Entering the surf first involved wading into the cresting waves. In those first few moments, the cold water only served to heighten my attention and sense of anticipation. My goal in this first phase was to move out past the white foamy breakers to the zone where the incoming waves swelled like baby mountains but were not yet white-capped.

As I moved farther from the shore the noise and din of the crowds on the beach was slowly silenced by the roar of the pounding surf. Society's clamor was replaced by the quiet splash of incoming sets of blue and green waves and the occasional cry of a herring gull flying overhead. As I ventured into deeper and deeper water, my feet would briefly lose touch with the bottom and my body would be slowly lifted up, then noiselessly dropped back down into a trough. Up and down, up and down, like a buoy, like being in zero gravity, rendering me nearly weightless.

In phase two, nearly all of my attention was focused forward,

straining to see above the undulating swells to determine which
might offer the most promising ride. The quiet of being beyond
the breakers, hypnotically treading on the salty brine, amplified
my focus. No troubling thoughts of ableism, bigotry, or shame in-
vaded my peace. Only one intrusive thought occasionally forced
its way into my consciousness and interrupted my reverie. Due
to my occasional panic of not seeing the bottom, my imagination
would conjure up visions of tiger sharks or great whites lurking unseen beneath me. For that I blamed Steven Spielberg and his damn
movie *Jaws*.

But the fear of a shark attack was soon pushed aside as I scanned
for incoming waves big enough to catapult me to shore. Bobbing up
and down, I'd float and float, up and down. The lull between waves
might last a minute, sometimes ten minutes. Usually in solitude,
I learned to judge the swells and patiently evaluate which one to
begin paddling ahead of. Often, I'd stroke furiously only to be lifted
up but then left behind on the backside of the lip of a cresting wave.
Then I'd have to turn away from shore and stroke back out to sea.
Once returned to the lineup area, I'd begin the careful watching all
over again. Soon all troubles and concerns about the outside world
faded away, leaving me in a Zen-like state of total concentration and
complete alertness. This was play at its purest.

Eventually, my diligence would be rewarded with the approach
of a generously sized wave as it peaked in height before me. Thus
began phase three. With powerful short strokes, I'd position myself
just in front of the pocket, the section of the swell just ahead of the
cresting lip. Then I'd feel the wave's power lift me up and launch me
forward. Quickly, I'd tuck into the shape of a sleek torpedo. Arms
out in front, legs pushed tightly together behind me, like Superman
I'd be rocketed forward ten yards, twenty yards, thirty, sometimes
even forty or fifty yards. The longer the ride, the higher my ecstasy
quotient rose, but also the harder it became to hold my breath. A
really good ride would carry me along in its foamy white embrace
right to the shore's edge, where I'd surface gasping for breath. A bad
wave (known as a "bomb") could grab me in its clutches and tumble
me like a sneaker in a clothes dryer. A bomb would heave me up ass

over teakettle and then pile-drive me headfirst into the bottom, re-plete with painfully sharp bits of broken seashells. A bad wave inev-itably left the inside of my bathing suit filled with sandy grit.

Yet, time and again, the risk of wiping out was quickly replaced by the lure of the next big wave. Standing up in the shallows at the end of a good ride, I'd shake myself off and charge back through the breakers, eager to repeat the process all over again. To avoid being battered by incoming walls of waves three to five feet high, I learned to duck-dive under them and then bob up on the other side, where I'd stroke back out to the lineup. Unnoticed by me, it was a master class in becoming resilient.

A half century later, standing on the edge of a roaring surf, I con-tinue to be drawn to the lure and power of the ocean. That moment when a wave crests and hurtles my body forward is still the closest I've come to the danger and exhilaration of flying. Looking back, I sense it was Mother Earth's way of teaching me a profound Spir-itual lesson—that it's possible to navigate choppy waters and still experience hope, joy, and ultimately peace. From the boardwalk at Camp Lighthouse to my encounter with the red-tailed hawk at Clark Tower and the sacred awe of my Temagami experience, Her benevolence has time and again blessed me with a sense of connec-tion to my larger family.

Afterword

Insights from *An Eye for an I*

WHAT FOLLOWS is a handful of "ahas" that came only after retrospectively studying my own life as well as the lives and insights of others. I hope you find one or two helpful in your own journey.

We can find spiritual healing through diverse paths and in different places. Some of us meditate, others participate in or create art. Others pray or go in search of holy sites. Each can assist in our search for meaning and help us find our life's purpose. Each of these paths share one other thing in common: they put us in touch with something greater than ourselves, what I call Spirit.

An Eye for an I tells the story of how I moved through blindness, bigotry, and mental illness thanks to repeated encounters with Mother Earth's spiritual guides. Some of the "ahas" I took from those moments began with the recognition that, as part of Earth's family, we are never truly alone. To learn and be in touch with gratitude I need only be open to experiencing nature whenever and however It may show itself. That can happen not just in the wilderness but also in cities, like in my story of Manhattan's Paley Park. Nature has also shown me that pain and suffering can be the manure that helped my Spirit grow. Ada Limón once asked, "What is it about noticing beauty that brings you out of yourself and returns you to yourself?" The beauty of Mother Earth continues to provide me with the element of awe that can lift up my Spirit, if I'm wise enough to let It in.

One early insight has to do with the myth of blindness as tragedy. I don't ever recall feeling my blindness was a catastrophe worthy of pity. Shortly after my surgery I was asked, "Aren't you glad you got your eyesight back? Isn't it a miracle?" Although it seemed a straightforward question, I didn't have an easy answer because it is a complicated question. Yes, having my eyesight restored was a blessing. But I want people to grasp that I was more disabled by my environment and the social discrimination of others than by my physical blindness. Of course, having eyesight makes many things accessible to me that weren't accessible when I was legally blind. In *Country of the Blind,* Andrew Leland quotes Laura Wolk: "Blindness is going to impose limits on me that it doesn't impose on a sighted person. In some ways life would be easier for me if I were sighted. Blindness is at once a nondefining characteristic and a serious disability. And I can hold those ideas simultaneously in my mind." But having been blind also gave me special entry into a world not often made privy to the sighted.

It is useful to remember that I'm just like you except that for a decade I couldn't see very well. When I was legally blind, I was owed no less respect, value, or dignity than that granted to the sighted me today. Leland writes, "The failure to appreciate this basic fact, that someone's difference does nothing to alter their humanity, is the wellspring of all discrimination, alienation and oppression."

My story is complicated because I wasn't simply legally blind. I was a Latino in an Anglo society that devalues Latinos. And I lived with mental illness in a society that treats mental illness more as a stigma to be hidden than as a medical condition needing understanding and attention. My blindness, Latinoness, and mental health story were and are inseparable, and all wrapped up into one complex bundle. The image from my Temagami vision quest that illustrated this complex relationship best was of people dancing in the final evening's spiral, hand in hand, pulling and pushing one another toward finding the center of their journey. That vision of weaving dancers encapsulates how blindness, Puerto Ricanness, and mental illness were woven together into a singular dance that moved me toward finding my Spiritual Center.

As both a community organizer and an educator, I've witnessed how, within the larger movement for social justice, disability often gets ignored or pushed to the sidelines. As someone who was both racially and sexually assaulted, I persevered thanks to a host of good people, fortunate events, and Mother Earth who came to my assistance. Yet a Department of Justice study from 2009 to 2014 found that people with disabilities were two and a half times as likely to experience violent attacks, including rape and sexual assault, as nondisabled people.

In *Time*, Rebekah Taussig says, "Disability expands into every possible corner and intersects with every other identity." Activist Justice Shorter observes, "There is no way to separate [my] Blackness from having a disability." According to Leland, this generation of disability activists increasingly believe that "Disability justice begins from a premise of intersectionality . . . the idea that the oppressions people experience because of race, sexuality, gender, class, and disability are all linked, inseparable forces that need to be fought together." I no longer perceive my blindness, Puerto Ricanness, and family's mental health struggles as separate parts of my identity. They are all interwoven into one fabric.

Rather than being abstract, intersectionality becomes very real if one considers that between 30 and 50 percent of those killed by police are disabled. From my own reading I think it's safe to conclude that many of those killed may have also suffered from mental illness.

In her essay, Taussig asks, "Instead of disability as a limitation, what if a lack of imagination was the actual barrier?" Activists of her generation advocate for a reorientation from the approach where disabled people are expected to squeeze into able-bodied people's world, and instead call on able-bodied people to inhabit the world of the disabled. The relationship of the interwoven topics of mental illness, race, and disability to the larger society is an evolving and necessary conversation about "Otherness" for those of us committed to social justice.

Bigotry on the basis of disability, race, and mental illness shares several things in common with other forms of intolerance, things like isolation and violence. Each relies on cultural stigmas, individual shame, and institutional and economic disempowerment. The visionary Audre Lorde pointed out more than four decades ago that "There is no hierarchy of oppressions." Given their many commonalities, I've found that working on disability has the potential to help address them all.

Yet you might wonder, in the face of this litany of intersecting oppressions, "What can one person do?" or "Where do I begin?" In "Resources: Seeing Beyond Our Blind Spots" at the end of this book I've selected a short set of readings for those who are interested in exploring a bit more deeply issues of disability, racism, mental illness, and intersectionality. I also share a model, the Looking-Glass Self, that has aided me in seeing the world through fresh eyes. It has encouraged me to begin to inhabit the world of the Other.

I leave you with an invitation to explore the idea of blind spots, a major obstacle to seeing our worlds more clearly.

Acknowledgments

So many contributed directly and indirectly to this memoir that I'm sad I will inevitably forget to mention some people. My debt begins with my life partner and spiritual compañera, Carolyn O'Grady. Her encouragement, support, patience (with my bellyaching), and excellent editing skills have lifted me up too many times to count. For more than ten years, Colleen Bell has been my weekly writing buddy, champion, and Accountability Meister. Making the transition from academic writer to memoir writer has required gifted teachers, including Natalie Goldberg, Mary Carroll Moore, and Carolyn Holbrook, among others. I am blessed with not one but two remarkable writing groups, my MISA memoir pals and my La Crosse Third-Thursday writer friends. These folks have, time and again, proven hugely helpful in providing both encouragement and critical feedback. A special shout-out to Joy Baker, Patty Wetterling, and Carolyn Holbrook for generously sharing their experiences of the publication process. I was encouraged in the writing of this memoir when I received an honorable mention in the Jade Ring Writing Contest sponsored by the Wisconsin Writers Association.

This memoir went through many drafts, and I am fortunate that it had excellent beta readers, including Deb Holtz, Joan Levy, Steven Botkin, Tom Scarseth, Lisa McClintock, and the late, great Ruben Rosario and Laura Rauscher. You folks rock! Over the years, several people pushed my thinking in new directions, including Harriet Copher Haynes, "Mindful" Joe Nelson, Ellen Tadd, Jason-Aeric Heunecke, and Lisa Heldke. The staff of the University of

Minnesota Press have been invaluable partners, and I owe a special debt to Erik Anderson, Emma Saks, and Madeleine Vasaly. Like child-rearing, writing a book takes a village, and I am blessed that I stumbled into one as brilliant, kind, and forgiving as mine.

Resources

Seeing Beyond Our Blind Spots

The blind French philosopher Jacques Lusseyran in *Against the Pollution of the I* observed, "The sighted are constantly diverted from total attention. So are the blind, but not to the same extent. For them, remaining attentive to one's blind spots is a practical necessity." I've said that blindness is not just something that happened to me. It's also something that happened for me. It is one of several gifts handed me, as are being Puerto Rican and living and coping with mental illness. Those gifts began a transformation from the blind "Eye" to a seeing "I." Not only am I regularly forced to identify my blind spots, I'm often forced to see new possibilities.

Blind spots are not confined to the physically blind. They are about not sensing the world fully. For both the blind and the sighted, to overcome our blind spots we have to be attentive with all of our senses. I once listened on National Public Radio to a talented deaf singer with an angelic voice who was a pure joy to experience. She explained how she sang into a balloon pressed against her lips to practice gauging her voice's tonal qualities. Even though she could not hear her own voice in the traditional sense, she said, "I'm sad for people with hearing because they are often unable to find the joy of sensing music through the realms of vibration and touch."

Some of my blind spots are definitely physical. Not seeing out of my left eye has caused me to accidentally walk into a bed corner or crash into a stranger who approached me from my "blind" spot. As a kid I could see just enough to enjoy playing on New York City's many concrete handball courts. The hot pink of the Pensy Pinkie handball was just bright enough for me to find it against the dull gray of the courts and tested my reaction time. But my fantasy of being a handball legend ended when other kids figured out that a sure way to beat me was a well-placed shot in the lower left quadrant of my field of vision. They could see my blind spot before I did.

But blind spots are not simply about physical limits. Once while talking with a friend about a change of presidents at his college, I asked, "What's his name?" Given my knowledge of higher education at the time, I assumed I'd recognize the name. Clearing his throat, my friend said, "Ha! And you're Mr. Diversity? Our new president is a woman." Back then I felt embarrassed, annoyed, defensive, and resentful that my sexist blind spot had been exposed.

Like a physical blind spot, bias can often be noticed by others but left unrecognized by those with the bias. Newer cars come equipped with a feature called blind-spot monitoring that enables drivers to be alerted when they are drifting sideways into an unseen car. I look back on my decades as an educator as helping supposedly sighted people learn to find and monitor their blind spots when dealing with the Other. That requires noticing my own biases related to racism, sexism (including transphobia), heterosexism, religious oppression, classism, ageism, and ableism.

Overcoming blind spots demands a willingness to admit that we each have mental constructs and implicit biases that limit our vision. These blind spots can be detrimental to ourselves, to others, or to both. Growing up as a young Latino in Catholic school, I internalized the negative, lowered expectations of some White nuns. The nuns' belief that I was "slow" and not very smart resulted in my acting out. As a consequence, I was inaccurately tracked into "special needs" classes.

More than a quarter century later, I was still wrestling with that blind spot as I struggled to successfully defend my dissertation and overcome those same internalized stereotypes. Reading Valerie Young, a social justice educator, convinced me that I suffered from what she calls Impostor Syndrome and what I call Imposter, Fraud, Fake Syndrome. Her observations grew from years of working with women who unconsciously internalized society's belief in male superiority and the corresponding false belief in female inferiority.

Overcoming one's blind spots is never a "one and done" proposition. On a recent Zoom call, a writing colleague referred to her spouse in telling a story. Not thinking, I asked, "What's his name?" to which she kindly corrected, "My spouse is a woman." This time I thanked my Zoom friend for correcting my blind spot about sexual orientation. Yep, you can teach an old dog new tricks.

When I was legally blind, I relied heavily on a magnifying glass to read small print. This became a metaphor for my visual limitation, and lenses became a looking glass for my life. Since then, I've sought new ways of recognizing how I perceive others as well as how others might perceive me. One needn't be blind to see the world more clearly. We need only to be open to sensing our world more fully by remembering that when one eye closes, another I can open.

One helpful approach for understanding the complexity of how we see, or don't see, our worlds is the Johari Window. Created by Joseph Luft and Harry Ingham, it offers a way to develop greater self-awareness and understanding about the nature of our blind spots. For me it has been a "looking glass" showing how I perceive myself and others, and how others may perceive me. Resembling a grid of four windows, it describes four distinct frames for understanding the differences between how we perceive ourselves and how others might perceive us.

The Johari Window

1 **The Known Self** Things we know about ourselves and others know about us: the "public self"	2 **The Blind Self** Things that others may know about us that we do not know; mannerisms, attitudes, or styles with which we compare ourselves to others
3 **The Hidden Self** Things we know about ourselves that others do not know unless we disclose them	4 **The Unknown Self** Things neither we nor others know about us, such as ignorance of our potential or of our biases

1. The first window is named The Known Self because
   we are able to see our own actions and those of people
   around us clearly, without obstruction or distortion. Here
   our attitudes, feelings, beliefs, skills, and views are well
   known to ourselves as well as to others. Children often
   see the world in openly unfiltered and unbiased ways.
   We've all heard adults comment how wonderful it could
   be to see the world "through the eyes of a child."

2. The second window is called The Blind Self. In this frame,
   our actions, attitudes, and information are known to
   others, but as individuals we aren't aware of our blind
   spots. Think back to me on the handball court and how I
   failed to see my blind spot. For those in privileged groups
   (e.g., the sighted), it isn't uncommon to be clueless about
   when people are behaving in ways that stereotype or
   limit opportunities for people in marginalized groups.
   Pitying the disabled may seem harmless to the sighted,
   but the disabled are keenly attuned to its negative
   repercussions. My sexist assumption that the new
   college president would be a male was another example
   of a blind spot. Interestingly, blind spots can also take the
   form of an individual being unaware of their potential.

3. The third window is the Hidden Self, or the Façade.
   Here actions and information about the individual
   are known by that individual but not to anyone else.
   Examples could include a person who is gay hiding their
   sexual orientation for safety's sake, or a working-class
   person pretending to be middle class to avoid being
   marginalized in certain settings. My reluctance to use my
   cane was a means of hiding my difference as a means of
   avoiding becoming vulnerable.

4. The last window is the Unknown Self. Here information
   and behaviors are unknown to the individual and also
   unseen by others. I developed some subconscious
   behaviors and implicit bias against some in the Black

and Latina community. My early preference for blond, blue-eyed White women coupled with my romantic avoidance of women of color went unnoticed for years, by both me and my partners. I did not recognize it as a blind spot or as a manifestation of my internalized racism. Not until I was able to surface those subconscious biases was I able to reexamine my own behavior and see others in a different light. Like in the Blind Self, a person's gifts or potential for greatness (e.g., as an artist, writer, performer, leader) may also go untapped if not recognized.

The premise behind using the Johari Window model as a looking glass is that our interactions shape how we see ourselves and others, and how people see us. When views align well, we can be more effective, engaging, and helpful, whether it be in a diverse team, work, or family setting. As we identify our blind spots, we begin visualizing the differences between how we see ourselves and how others might perceive us. It's not easy because it requires that we capture our thoughts about who we are, and then get feedback from others on how we are perceived. Some examples of the usefulness of feedback are how writers often gather in small groups to receive 360-degree feedback on their work or how women, men, and people of color can gather in affinity groups to unpack their blind spots.

Here is a list of introductory resources for those interested in exploring these topics further.

Mental Health

If you or a loved one is struggling with notions of self-harm, the National Suicide and Crisis Lifeline offers twenty-four-hour assistance by calling or texting 988. English, Spanish, and other languages are available.

Atlas, Galit, PhD. *Emotional Inheritance: A Therapist, Her Patients, and the Legacy of Trauma.* Little, Brown Spark, 2022.
Foo, Stephanie. *What the Bones Know: A Memoir of Healing from Complex Trauma.* Ballantine Books, 2022.

Blindness

Bruni, Frank. *The Beauty of Dusk: On Vision Lost and Found.* Avid Reader Press, 2022.

Godin, M. Leona. *There Plant Eyes: A Personal and Cultural History of Blindness.* Pantheon Books, 2021.

Leland, Andrew. *The Country of the Blind: A Memoir of the End of Sight.* Penguin Press, 2023.

Lusseyran, Jacques. *Against the Pollution of the I: On the Gifts of Blindness, the Power of Poetry, and the Urgency of Awareness.* New World Library, 2006.

Disability

Clare, Eli. *Brilliant Imperfection: Grappling with Cure.* Duke University Press, 2017.

Crip Camp: A Disability Revolution. Documentary available from Higher Ground Productions; first released on Netflix March 25, 2020.

Heumann, Judith, with Kristen Joiner. *Being Heumann: An Unrepentant Memoir of a Disability Rights Activist.* Beacon Press, 2023.

Taussig, Rebekah. *Sitting Pretty: The View from My Ordinary Resilient Disabled Body.* Harper One, 2020.

Exploring Whiteness and Racism

DiAngelo, Robin. *White Fragility: Why It's So Hard to Talk to White People About Racism.* Beacon Press, 2018.

Daniel Tatum, Beverly. *Why Are All the Black Kids Sitting Together in the Cafeteria? and Other Conversations About Race.* Twentieth Anniversary Edition (revised and updated). Beacon Press, 2017.

Intersectionality

For an introduction to the topic of intersectionality, see the short film *Kids Explain Intersectionality* at https://www.youtube.com/watch?v=WzbADY-CmTs.

To further explore intersectionality, watch *Intersectionality and Disability*: https://www.youtube.com/watch?v=p2XNoCQazro.

References

Adams Maurianne, Lee Anne Bell, and Pat Griffin, editors. *Teaching for Diversity and Social Justice*, 2nd edition. Taylor and Francis Group, 2007.

Atlas, Galit, PhD. *Emotional Inheritance: A Therapist, Her Patients, and the Legacy of Trauma*. Little, Brown Spark, 2022.

Bennett, Britt. *The Vanishing Half.* Riverhead Books, 2020.

Blind Works. "Famous People with Visual Impairments." Accessed November 3, 2022. https://brailleworks.com/braille-resources/famous-people-with-visual-impairments.

Bonilla, J. "Redefining Machismo." *Colors* 4, no. 3 (May–June 1995), 8–11. Minneapolis.

Bregman, Rutger. *Humankind: A Hopeful History*. Little, Brown and Company, 2019.

Brown, Brené. *Atlas of the Heart: Mapping Meaningful Connections and the Language of Human Experience*. Random House, 2021.

Bruni, Frank. *The Beauty of Dusk: On Vision Lost and Found*. Avid Reader Press, 2022.

Clare, Eli. *Brilliant Imperfection: Grappling with Cure*. Duke University Press, 2017.

Cleaver, Eldridge. *Soul on Ice*. Ramparts Press, 1968.

Crip Camp: A Disability Revolution. Higher Ground Productions. Released on Netflix March 25, 2020.

Dirlikov, E., et al. "Tuberculosis Surveillance and Control, Puerto Rico, 1898–2015." *Emerging Infectious Diseases*. Accessed June 2, 2022. http://doi.org/10.3201/eid2503.181157.

Foo, Stephanie. *What the Bones Know: A Memoir of Healing from Complex Trauma*. Ballantine Books, 2022.

Godin, M. Leona. *There Plant Eyes: A Personal and Cultural History of Blindness*. Pantheon Books, 2021.

Goldberg, Nicholas. "The Urban Legend of Kitty Genovese and the 38 Witnesses Who Ignored Her Blood-Curdling Screams." *Los Angeles Times*, September 10, 2020.

Goldfarb, David, and Marty Ford. "Lifeline for People with Disabilities Forces Them to Live in Poverty." *The Hill*. Accessed October 25, 2022. https://thehill.com/opinion/congress-blog/3702528-lifeline-for -people-with-disabilities-forces-them-to-live-poverty/.

Gornick, Vivian. "'Put on the Diamonds': Notes on Humiliation." *Harper's Magazine*, October 2021. Accessed October 16, 2022. https://harpe rs.org/archive/2021/10/put-on-the-diamonds-notes-on-humiliation -vivian-gornick/.

Gottlieb, Laura. *Maybe You Should Talk to Someone: A Therapist, Her Therapist, and Our Lives Revealed*. Houghton Mifflin Harcourt Publishing Company, 2019.

Huemann, Judith, and John Wodatch. "We're 20% of America and We're Still Invisible" (2020). Accessed October 15, 2022. http://nytimes .com/2020/07/26/opinion/2020/Americans-with-disabilities-act. html.

Kennedy, Robert F. Day of Affirmation Address (June 6, 1966). University of Capetown, South Africa.

Kreskow, Kelly. *Overrepresentation of Minorities in Special Education*. St. John's College Education Masters. Paper 257. 2013. Accessed October 16, 2022. https://fisherpub.sjf.edu/education_ETD_masters/257/.

Leland, Andrew. *The Country of the Blind: A Memoir of the End of Sight*. Penguin Press, 2023.

Lorde, Audre. "There Is No Hierarchy of Oppressions." *Homophobia and Education Bulletin*. Council on Interracial Books for Children, 1983. Accessed September 4, 2023. https://theanarchistlibrary.org/library/ audre-lorde-there-is-no-hierarchy-of-oppressions.

Luelmo, Paul, and Dustin Bindreiff. "The Disproportionality of Latinx Students in Special Education: The Growing Need to Build Relationships." *Leadership Magazine* (January–February 2021). The Association of California School Administrators. Accessed October 26, 2022.

https://leadership.acsa.org/disproportionality-of-latinx-students
-special-ed.

Luft, Joseph, and Harry Ingham. The Johari Window Model. Accessed
October 10, 2022. https://www.communicationtheory.org/the-johari
-window-model/.

Lusseyran, Jacques. Against the Pollution of the I: On the Gifts of Blindness,
the Power of Poetry, and the Urgency of Awareness. New World Library,
2006.

Mate, Gabor. The Myth of Normal: Trauma, Illness, and Healing in a Toxic
Culture. Avery, 2022.

Moorjani, Anita. Facebook, September 2, 2023. https://www.facebook
.com/photo.php?fbid=745214020294428&id=100044175112268&set
=a,2599004790025355.

Morton, Brian. Tasha: A Son's Memoir. Avid Reader Press, 2022.

O'Neil, Cathy. Shame Machine: Who Profits in an Age of Humiliation.
Crown Publishing, 2022.

Rivera, Magaly. "Puerto Rico's History (1950–2022)." Welcome to Puerto
Rico! Accessed October 16, 2022. https://welcome.topuertorico.org/
history6.shtml.

Smith, Jessica. "Half Human, Half Robot." Time Magazine. (August 14,
2023).

Smith, Zadie. Swing Time. Hamish Publishing, 2016.

Taussig, Rebekah. "I've Been Paralyzed Since I Was 3: Here's Why Kindness Toward the Disabled Is More Complicated Than You Think."
Time, August 31, 2020.

Taussig, Rebekah. Sitting Pretty: The View from My Ordinary Resilient Disabled Body. Harper One, 2020.

Vélez, W. "The Educational Experiences of Puerto Ricans in the United
States." In H. Rodríguez, R. Sáenz, and C. Menjívar, editors, Latina/
os in the United States: Changing the Face of América. Springer Science
and Business Media, 2008.

Wall Kimmerer, Robin. Braiding Sweetgrass: Indigenous Wisdom, Scientific
Knowledge, and the Teaching of Plants. Milkweed Editions, 2015.

Wikipedia. "New Jersey Pine Barrens." Accessed October 25, 2022.
https://en.wikipedia.org/wiki/New_Jersey_Pine_Barrens.

Wright, Winthrop R. Café con Leche: Race, Class, and National Image in
Venezuela. University of Texas Press, 1993.

Young, Valerie. *The Secret Thoughts of Successful Women: Why Capable People Suffer from the Impostor Syndrome and How to Thrive in Spite of It*. Crown Publishing, 2011.

Zacharek, Stephanie. "An Obamas-Produced Doc Takes Viewers Inside the Birth of the Disability Rights Movement." *Time*, March 25, 2020.

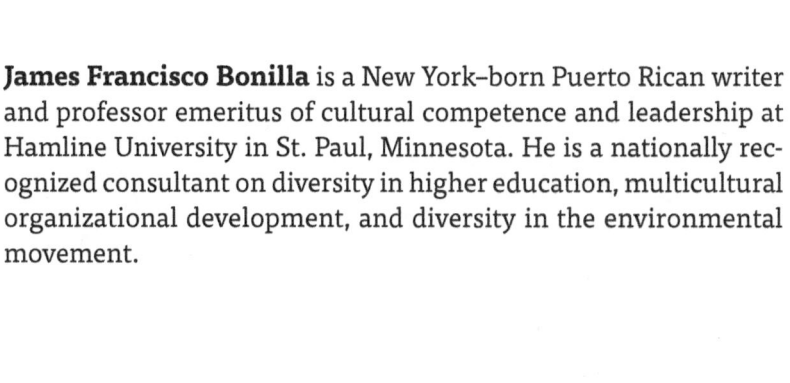

James Francisco Bonilla is a New York–born Puerto Rican writer and professor emeritus of cultural competence and leadership at Hamline University in St. Paul, Minnesota. He is a nationally recognized consultant on diversity in higher education, multicultural organizational development, and diversity in the environmental movement.